WARP SPEED WINDOWS

WARP SPEED WINDOWS

David Field

M&T BOOKS

M&T Books
A Division of MIS:Press
A Subsidiary of Henry Holt and Company, Inc.
115 West 18th Street
New York, New York 10011

© 1993 by M&T Books

Printed in the United States of America

Field, David, 1944 May 25
Warp Speed WIndows / David Field.
p. cm.
Includes index
ISBN 1-55851-327-2 :
1. Windows (Computer programs) I. Title
QA76.76W56F54 1993   93-39129
005.4'3—dc20   CIP

ISBN: 1-55851-327-2

Publisher: Steve Berkowitz
Associate Publisher: Brenda McLaughlin
Development Editor: Margot Owens Pagan
Production Editor: Mark Masuelli
Associate Production Editor: Joseph McPartland
Copy Editor: Edward Hogan
Technical Editor: Alexander M. Pagan

To Liz, for everything else

Table of Contents

Acknowledgments xv

Why This Book is For You 1

Introduction 3

Section I: Instant Gratification 11

Chapter I: Cleaning Up Your Desktop 13

Chapter 2: Advanced Desktop 29

Chapter 3: Using Windows Multitasking 51

Section II: For People Who Read Instructions 63

Chapter 4: Hardware 65

Who's who in the Market 66

Why Computers Run Fast or Slow 67

Which Chip is Which? 68

Computers No, Data Processing Yes 68

What's On the Motherboard 69

Why Video Cards Are Important 70

Cache Memory—Enough Will Do 71

The hit and miss world of caches 72

What's Different About Your Computer? Nothing 73

The Need for Speed 74

How Long Will You Run This Computer? 75

You may need more computer than you think 75

Choosing the Dream Machine 76

Buying a new computer 77

How to rate them 77

Why you don't need a large cache 78

RAM—not enough will slow you down 79

Hard Drives—knowing what counts 80

Why your TEMP directory is important 81

Video—Local Bus, VESA, and other terms you should know 82

Colors, Resolution *and* Speed 83

Summary 84

Software that can slow you down 85

Keep your disk defragmentized 86

Check the Turbo button! 86

Benchmarks Aren't Always Right..87

How to make a slow computer "faster".......................88

My computer's faster than your computer...................88

Anyone for Snake Oil?...89

Upgrades That Are Worthwhile...90

The Bottom Line on Fast...91

Chapter 5: Why Windows works the way it does— and how to exploit it..93

It's not DOS with Pretty Pictures...94

Too much versatility?..95

The "Secret" Is That There Are No Secrets.............................96

The magical "SetWindowsSpeed=0.5" line.................97

What's happening in Windows...98

Sizing windows..98

Get Some Hands On...100

Where did my program go..103

Programs as icons..105

Memos and Dialog Boxes...106

Finding Out More About Your Programs................................107

Windows Control Panel..108

Working Faster in File Manager..114

Copying from diskettes..115

Chapter 6: Keeping Your Desktop Organized.......................117

Why your Desktop is in a Mess..119

Cleaning Up the Mess..120

Improving the setup...120

What you see When You Start Up 121

    Keeping it neat 122

The next step 123

    Cascading windows 123

    Tiling windows 124

    Improving Tiling 125

The Secret of Setting Up Program Manager 125

    Retrieving icons 125

    Creating your most important group 127

    Accommodating other people 128

    The next most important program group 129

    Using Properties 130

    Now your files can have forty-character names 133

    Getting an Icon Back 134

Chapter 7: Advanced Desktop, with File Icons and a Handy Clock 137

The Different Kinds of Data Files 137

    File icons - OK in small doses 139

    File icons with long names 140

Making File Icons 140

    The slower (but easier) method 141

    Adding a long name 144

    The faster (but more complex) method 146

    Using the DOS Path 148

File Icon Tips and Tricks 148

Associating Files with Applications 149

    Association tips and tricks 150

Exploiting the Start Up Group 152

Improving a Desktop 153

Changing Clock's settings...154

Chapter 8: How Windows Accessories can Speed your Work 155

Write 156

Notepad 156

Object Packager 157

Media Player 160

Clock 161

Sound Recorder..161

Recorder 161

Paintbrush 162

Terminal 163

Calendar and Cardfile 164

Calculator 166

Character Map 167

Chapter 9: Unleashing the Power of Multitasking................171

A different kind of multitasking 172

Exploiting Windows multitasking 173

What does multitasking let you do? 174

Cool working with the cool switch 175

Problems with Alt+Tab 177

Getting Set for Better Multitasking 178

Adding RAM 178

Virtual Memory 179

The Permanent Swap File 180

    Setting up a Swap File 181

    Getting the correct sized swap file...........................183

Multitasking and the StartUp Group................................184

    Choosing programs for the StartUp group 184

    Making programs run minimized.............................186

The Alt+Tab way of life 187

Chapter 10: Speeding Through Windows Applications 189

Program Features to Speed You Up..................................194

Cut and Paste and Search and Replace............................198

OLE (Object Linking and Embedding)............................199

Chapter 11: Beyond Windows: Working with Desktop Shells..........................203

PC Tools for Windows 204

    The PC Tools Desktop..204

Using PC Tools to Improve Productivity 206

    File Manager 206

    Miscellaneous Tools 207

    Quick Launch 208

    Configuring Quick Launch.......................................208

    Configuring Quick Launch with Multiple File Windows..........209

Exploring PC Tools...211

Chapter 12: Crash and Burn 213

Making Your Machine as Stable as Possible.....................214

    More RAM 214

UPS and Other Power Line Protection.......................215

Tape Backup 217

Expansion Card Overload..................................217

Don't run with the cover off...............................218

Disk compression – a danger? 218

Planning to avert disaster 219

Using Timed Backups and Other File Strategies.......219

Virus Checking..220

Save at Appropriate Times 221

Disk Recovery Systems 221

General Protection Faults....................................221

What the Messages Mean.................................221

What You Should Do 222

Incompatibility...223

Dr. Watson...223

BOOTLOG.TXT 224

Recovering from a crash 224

Checking the TEMP Directory 225

Chapter 13: Warp Speed to the Future.....................227

What We Want From an Operating System....................228

The Future of Windows 229

Windows NT 230

Windows 4.0..231

Win 32s...233

Windows at Work 233

Windows alternatives...234

The Future of Hardware 234

Non-Intel machines 235

Power PC 235

Intel chips..236

OLE 2.0 237

Automated OLE..237

How To Run Any Computer at Warp Speed 239

It's Not the Computer, It's The Operator..................................240

Acknowledgments

This book had its genesis in a series of articles I wrote for the Boston Computer Society's IBM Group publication, *PC Report*. I'd like to thank Ellen Siever and Nancy Woolford for giving me the opportunity. I'd also like to thank Art Torrey and Darius Thabit for giving me plenty of technical help via the IBM Group's bulletin board.

Thanks also to Brenda McLaughlin of M & T for believing that the book had potential, and Steve Berkowitz of MIS Press in continuing with the project after MIS took over M & T. Special thanks to Margot Owens Pagan who pried this book away from me, chapter by chapter, using the "Margot Guilt Method."

With any book I write, there are always two special people to remember. One is to Roger Parker, who has been the utmost help professionally as well as being a very dear friend. The other thanks must go to my wife, Liz; in return for her support, she has suffered the destruction of our social life thanks to my inability to schedule properly. It'll be better next time, I promise.

Why This Book is For You

This book isn't about Windows – it's about you, and the way you work in the program. Other books give you a confusing range of options; this book shows you the quickest way to set up Windows so that you work faster. Follow the instructions in the Instant Gratification section and you'll be more productive—I guarantee it.

If you want to know more, or you're the person that's happiest with a full explanation, read the text. You'll find out why I chose the techniques I use and what methods to avoid. There are also many other tips in this section.

Whatever method you use, you'll suddenly realize that you're in charge—not Windows. You'll move faster and be more confident, working with the program instead of against it. And isn't that what computing is all about?

Introduction

This guy goes to the doctor.

"Well, Doc," he says brightly, "how are the results of those tests you ran on me?"

The doc gives him a grim look. "I have some bad news, and some very very bad news."

"Wow," says the guy, "what's the bad news?"

"You have twenty-four hours to live."

"Whew! . . .er, so what's the very very bad news?"

"I should have told you this yesterday."

I have some bad news, some very very bad news, and a little bit of good news.

The bad news is that any money you invest in new hardware and software is never going to make any more than a marginal improvement in your productivity.

The very very bad news is that the factor that you're ignoring, the one thing that slows you down more than anything, can only ever be improved by a small amount.

The little bit of good news is that this book tells you how to do exactly that.

The glossy ad in my computer magazine promises the earth. With this manufacturer's new machine, which features a Local Bus graphic accelerator, ". . . you'll work up to fifty times faster!"

I want a computer like that. I want one which lets me do a week's work in just over three-quarters of an hour, so I can lie in the sun for the rest of the time. Will this machine let me do this? Of course not.

How does this five thousand percent improvement translate into reality? In a typical workweek, someone using this machine might save a couple of minutes. That's less than a tenth of a one percent increase—hardly "fifty times faster!"

We are confusing machine power with overall productivity. We place our faith in the next breakthrough in technology, which will somehow catapult us into increased productivity, while all the time ignoring the real reason why we work so slowly.

What is it, this logjam? Why doesn't anyone pay attention to it? Can you see it? Yes, you can. If you look a few inches to left and right of where you're reading now, you'll see its thumbs.

In Pogo's immortal words, "We have met the enemy, and he is us."

We use our computers interactively—we do something, the computer reacts, the computer does something else, we react. While we demand instant response from our computer, we don't do it the same favor.

Because we're ill-prepared and move slowly, we hold up the computer far more than it holds us up. It's difficult to imagine how fast a computer moves compared to human reactions: here's some examples.

In the early seventies, I was told that when a speedy typist is entering data into the computer, you can imagine that, to the computer, the time between each click is similar to the amount of time you spend reading a chapter of this book. A good typist makes six keypresses a second.

At around the same time, I was programming computers to support multiple users. The computer was controlled by a program called the executive, which checked every terminal and every peripheral to see if users' individual programs needed attention. Otherwise, while it was waiting for a new keypress or the end of some printing, the computer would loop round and round the executive, waiting for something to do.

This arrangement seemed to work fine for the ten or twelve users that the system was designed to support, but one of the engineers checked to see how much time the computer actually ran programs and how long it stayed in the executive. Servicing multiple users, with seventies technology, the computer spent ninety-eight percent of its time in the executive, waiting for the humans.

What about today's technology? Let's suppose you get a dialog box on your screen, asking you to choose between OK and Cancel. This is similar to a branch instruction in computer instructions; both circumstances are asking you or the computer to choose an action based on a prevailing condition.

I'd guess that you'd take between one and two seconds to respond to this box by moving the mouse so that the cursor covered one or the other button, and pressing the mouse button. The computer responds to this type of situation about fifteen million times faster.

It's hard to understand what "fifteen million times faster" actually means, but here's an attempt. Technology like computers has enabled us to extend our physical powers. Unaided, we can walk all day at three miles an hour; or we can use technology in the form of a jet airliner. This lets us move two hundred times faster than walking speed, at nearly six hundred miles an hour.

In the time it takes for a human to walk about fifteen miles, a jet can fly across the USA, nearly 3,000 miles. What would happen if our jet was fifteen million times faster than walking speed? It would cross the USA before we'd finished our first step.

Do you want a computer that's twice as fast as the one you've got? It would run thirty million times faster than you. You wouldn't respond any faster. In fact, it's merely when disk accesses and printing slow down the CPU that we notice our computer is making us wait. Only high-end photomanipulation programs begin to tax the processor itself; all the rest of the time it has power way beyond our needs.

So any increase in CPU power is superfluous, except for when it speeds up disk access and printing. When these processes are speeded up, as they surely will be, then the whole computer will appear to obey every command instantaneously.

Will we be prepared? Of course not. We'll still have our reaction time, we'll still have our inefficient ways of working, and we'll still stop and wonder what to do next. And most of all, we'll still be waiting for a faster computer in the hopes that it will make us more productive.

Let's move from theory to a (fictitious) practice. Bob and Betty both work for Gigantic Developments; Bob is a power user, Betty looks on her computer like a typewriter or a copier. Bob has the very latest machine; Betty gets whatever she's given. The last time I looked, Bob had a 486-66 with every RAM slot filled, local bus accelerated video, you name it—he had it. Betty had a 386 SX.

Because Bob is a power user, he makes a point of having most of those thick, heavy books on Windows, and spends a lot of his time tweaking the system. Whenever anything new comes out, Bob gets to try it. If Bob says that It Is Good, then everyone smiles, and the lucky few around the company also get it.

Betty was shown how to use Windows by the woman who had the job before her. She doesn't know what's inside the box, what a power user is, how to adjust her time slicing. Yet, as you probably guessed, Betty is more productive than Bob.

There are several reasons why this is so. Betty can type; Bob still uses two fingers. A two-page report takes Bob half an hour, and Betty only fifteen minutes. Bob's spell checker is about ten seconds faster than Betty's, and he gains two or three seconds when he opens the program and saves his document.

Bob is an important person. He's on the phone much of the time; he regularly goes to meetings. Every second he spends away from his computer costs him millions of operations. He's never worked out whether he should go to all these meetings, or take and make all those phone calls; when he has to come in on Saturdays to get his work done, he seems to achieve so much more.

Betty spends most of her day at her desk. She chats occasionally with the people around her, and gets and makes a call or two to her friends. Yet she still gets her work finished at the end of the day.

Bob was a power user back in the DOS days, and he knew every keyboard shortcut going. He still uses keyboard commands, claiming they're much faster than using the mouse. Yet he often stops to look up the keystrokes for an extended character, like an accent, in one of the big books he has by his machine.

Betty was shown how to use the methods outlined in this book; she doesn't know how to run Windows any other way. Even by using Character Map she can put in an accent about five times faster than Bob.

Bob is in love with computers; Betty couldn't care less. Yet in just about every way Betty is more efficient, but then, she doesn't see what's so bad about learning to type, organizing yourself, and concentrating on just the things you really need to know. Bob adores having the latest and greatest on his desk, just like you. But don't be ashamed. Deep down, in my heart of hearts, I'm a Bob too.

Multiply Bob and Betty by all the people using computers at work, and you begin to get a discouraging picture. There was a lot of fuss recently when a study showed that in spite of the widespread adoption of personal computers in business, office productivity had not risen in years.

It's not difficult to see why. Five years ago, Bob's computer might have been only two million times faster than him. He could have wasted hundredths of a second several dozen times a day. Thanks to present-day technology, he's saved that.

Here's an even bigger paradox. Top-of-the-line computers of today are as powerful as the average mainframe computer of seven years ago. Seven years ago, Gigantic Developments had fifty terminals attached to its mainframe. Now it has two hundred PCs—some are older and less powerful models, but it's still over a hundred-fold increase in computing power. I think you can see by now why that figure has little impact on productivity.

Upgrading to a newer, faster computer is like trading in the family sedan for a sports car and still forgetting where you put your keys. Computer power is more than ample; no increase is going to have more than an insignificant increase in productivity.

By focusing on the less glamorous issues like user skills, more efficient working conditions, and, for what it's worth, the methods outlined in this book, real productivity can be achieved. Perhaps we'll lose our infatuation with computer speed, and concentrate on the areas no-one is measuring.

If you still can't give up that sexy machine of your dreams, consider this: How will we know when the computer is fast enough? When it keeps us waiting for nothing.

That's when we'll keep it waiting for everything.

Click.

Instant Gratification

For people who start tinkering before they read instructions

Cleaning Up Your Desktop

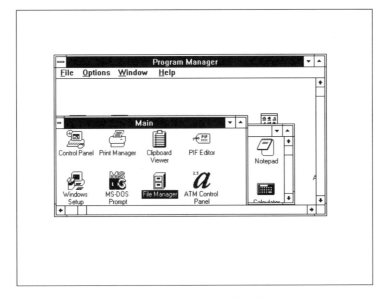

Is this the way your screen looks when you open Windows? Did you pay for a beautiful fourteen inch color monitor but only use half of it? How do you get an application to start? What applications are installed? The desktop pictured above isn't functional. It needs far too much work to do anything.

Restore

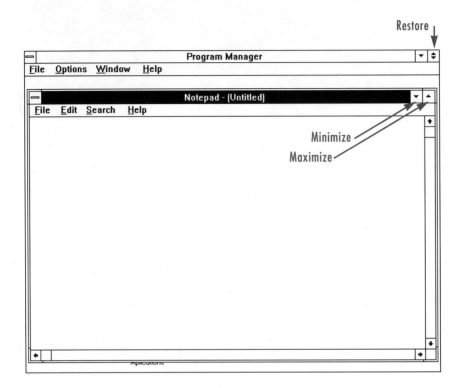

Program Manager

File   Options   Window   Help

Notepad - (Untitled)

File   Edit   Search   Help

Minimize

Maximize

Aplications

2 The Maximize and Minimize buttons (the arrowheads in the upper right-hand corner of the screen) let you change the size of your windows. **Maximize** will make the window fill the screen; **Restore** changes the window to an intermediate size, and **Minimize** changes the window into an icon. You should Maximize Program Manager to use all the space on the monitor. You can clean up the screen by Minimizing all the open windows.

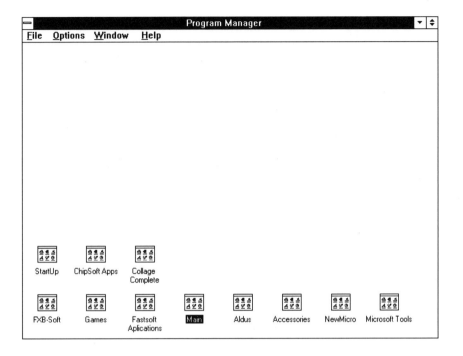

3 Now here's a better arrangement, although it's hardly perfect. For instance, you can't tell which applications are installed, however, you can make a reasonable guess as to where to find them. For example, if you've used Windows before, you'll expect to find File Manager in the Main group. However, every time you open Windows, you can't start applications directly—you have to open a window first.

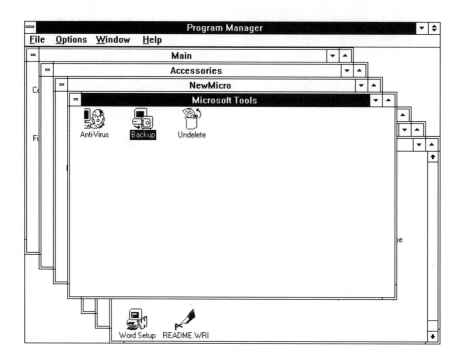

4 Another solution is to have all the windows open, so that you can see the icons that actually start an application. This method is called **Cascade,** and it's the least useful way of arranging your open windows. To get your screen looking this way, open all the group windows, then choose **Cascade** from the Window menu. The problem with Cascade is that you can only fully see one window at a time.

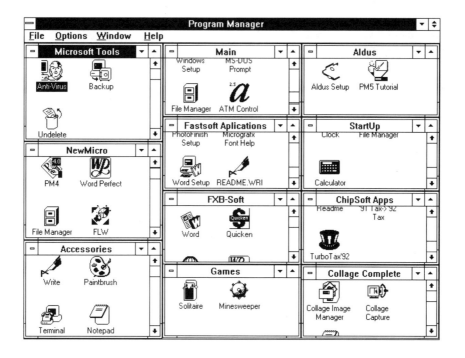

5 This is better—it's called **Tiling.** Open all your group windows and choose **Tile** from the Program Manager window menu. You'll get several windows that will be as large as possible without obstructing anything. However, some windows have plenty of space and only a few icons, while others have so many icons you can't see them all at once.

Instant Gratification

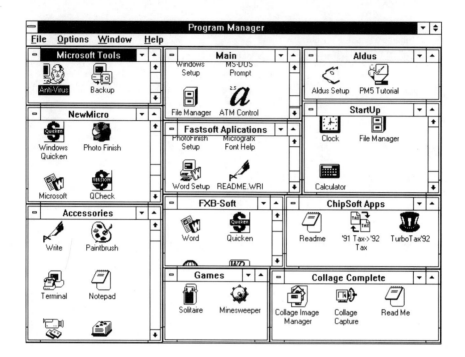

6 By reducing the size of some of the windows with only a few icons—making more space in the windows that are heavily populated—you'll get the best arrangement possible with Tiling. This method still doesn't address all the problems; there are too many icons to fit in any arrangement of Tiled windows. Also, what will you do if you add new applications?

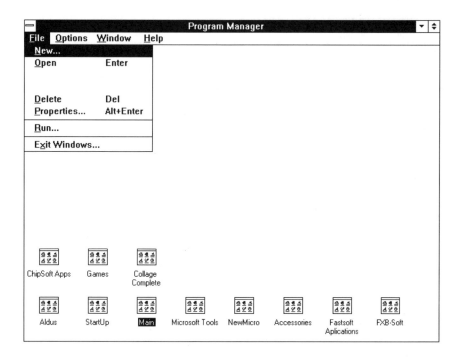

7 One problem with all the previous methods is that they assume you'll want to keep all your icons on display. The only icons you really need are the ones that start programs; the rest can be hidden away. Why keep Installer or Read Me icons cluttering your desktop? Start by creating a new group. Go to the File Menu in Program Manager and select **New.**

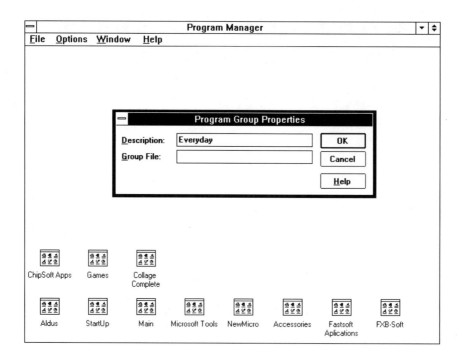

8 Choose a new **Program Group,** and click **OK.** You should be seeing the dialog box above. Type in a description in **Description** you can have up to forty characters with full punctuation and spaces, if you need them. Give this new group a name like **Everyday,** because this is where you'll keep the icons that you use all the time. You don't need to enter anything in the Group File box.

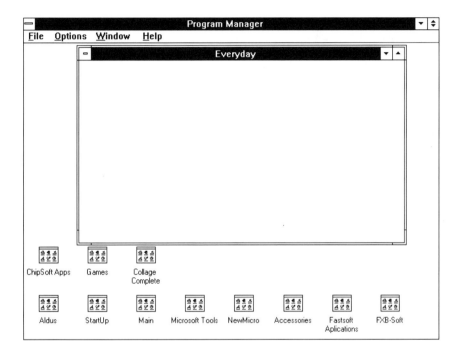

9 Here's the empty group window for Everyday. This window will be open whenever you start Windows, and it will contain all your application icons visible and ready to double-click. By dealing with icons, instead of windows, you'll cut down on your desktop clutter, make obvious which applications you have and where to find them, and generally save time.

Instant Gratification

21

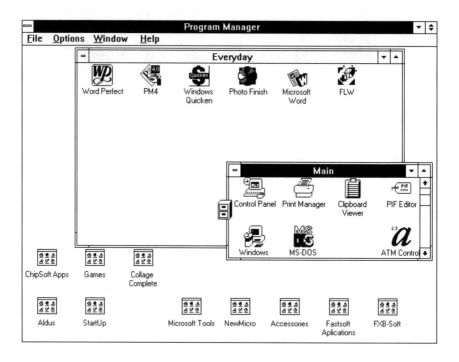

10 Now open each of your current windows individually and drag the icons that start the programs you use frequently into Everyday. Leave the Install and ReadMe icons behind. Don't move icons you think you *might* need; just move the icons you know you'll use. Don't drag in any applications from the Accessories group for the moment; on the next page you'll see what to do with File Manager once you dragged it into Everyday.

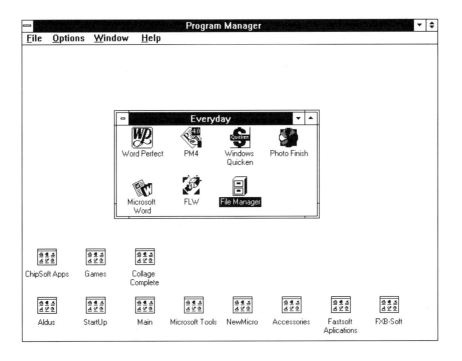

11 Here's the completed Everyday group window, with your favorite applications and File Manager. You use File Manager so often, it's worth keeping in Everyday. However, if someone else uses your machine, they may be dismayed to find File Manager is missing from the Main window. To get around this, hold down the **Control** key as you drag the File Manager icon into Everyday. This makes it possible to copy it into the Everyday window and leave the original behind. When you've filled Everyday, size the window to fit the icons, and position it centrally on the screen.

Instant Gratification

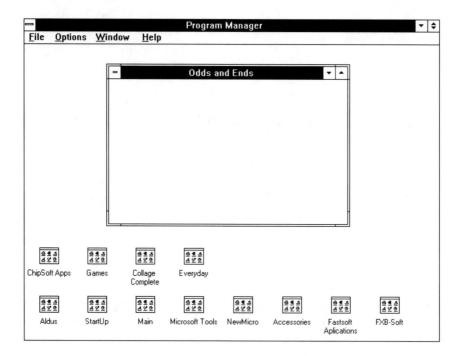

12 Now follow the same procedure you used to create the Everyday window to make another group window called **Odds and Ends**. This is the place for all the icons that are left in the program groups created by applications. Leave the Main, Accessories, Startup, and Games groups alone for the moment.

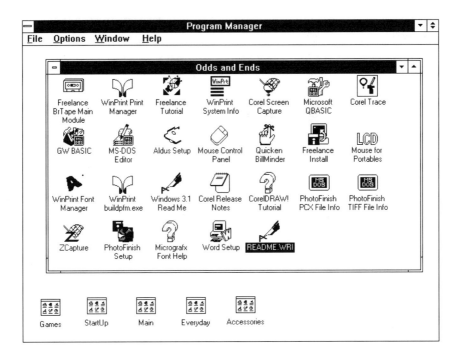

13 Here's the completed Odds and Ends group, containing all the leftover icons you'll probably never use again. If you do, you'll know where to find them—not in groups created by applications messing up your desktop. When those group windows are completely emptied, go to the File menu and choose **Delete.** Relax! You can't delete anything but icons and windows in Program Manager.

Instant Gratification

25

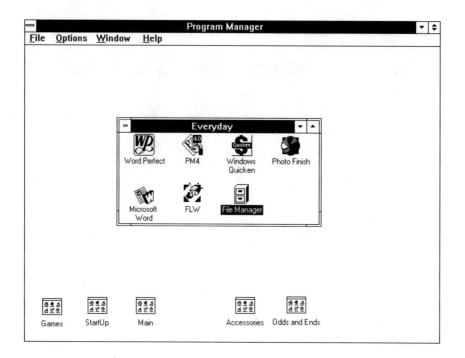

14 Here's your new desktop! This is the only way you'll see Program Manager from now on if you followed steps 1-13. You won't ever have to dig around in windows looking for icons, or remember which window a particular application icon was in. Notice, also, that you have very few other group windows, now that you've consolidated your icons. If you install a new program (application), just move the appropriate icon to Everyday and Odds and Ends, and delete the group window that the program created.

Instant Gratification

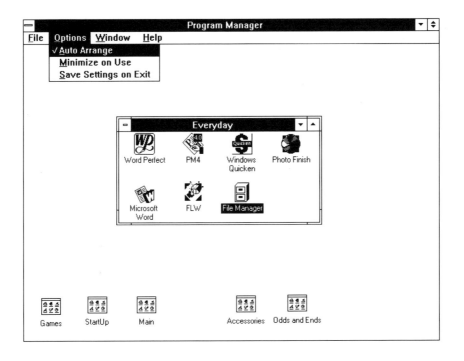

15 To keep your desktop looking this way from now on, go to the Options menu in Program Manager. Click on **Auto Arrange,** and click on (unchecking) **Save Settings on Exit** this only if it has a checkmark next to it. Now hold down the **Shift** key and go to **Exit Windows** on the File menu. You won't exit Windows, but your settings will be saved until you change them again by using the **Shift-Exit Windows** method.

Advanced Desktop

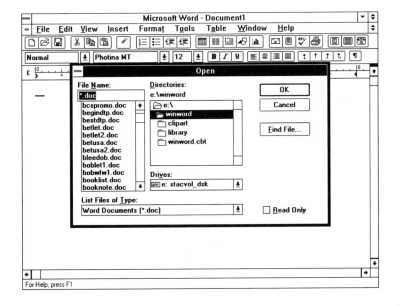

Is this how you expect files to open? Do you have trouble remembering exactly what SCRDENGS.DOC contains? Windows isn't the best operating system to keep control of your files, but it has surprising powers which make keeping track of your work much simpler. Your desktop can be the way to open applications and files at the same time, without going through dialog boxes like this.

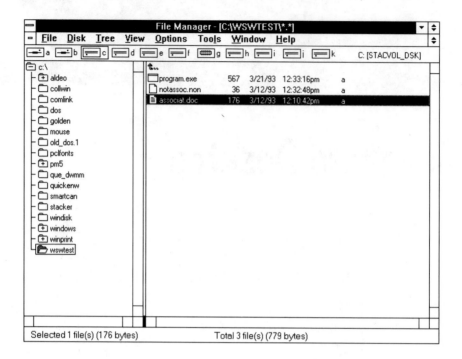

2 File Manager is one way of opening files and the applications (programs) that create them. In this example, PROGRAM.EXE is an application and clicking on this icon makes it run. Under Windows, files can be associated with an application, so clicking on a file icon in File Manager will open the file as well as start the program. This is the status of ASSOCIAT.DOC; clicking on this icon will start Word for Windows and open the file. The final file, NOTASSOC.NON, is not associated with (linked to) any program.

30

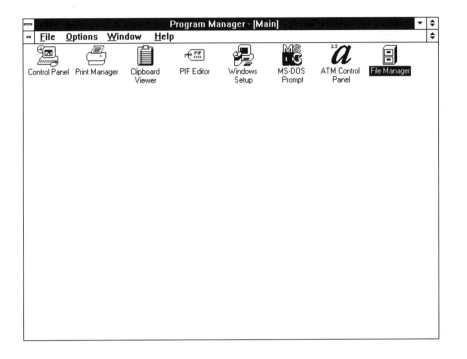

3 You can use the power of association to create icons in Program Manager that will both run a program and open a file simultaneously (you'll see how to make an association later in this section). What's more, you can give the new icon up to forty characters of description, including all punctuation and spaces. Start in Program Manager by opening the Main group window, and use the Maximize button so that the window fills the screen.

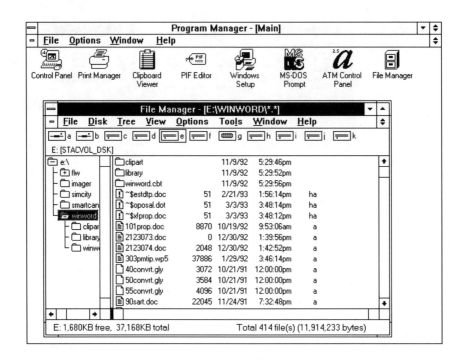

4 Now open File Manager by double-clicking on its icon. It will probably open full-screen and hide Program Manager. If it does, press on the **Restore** button, so File Manager *floats* above Program Manager, as in the figure above. It doesn't matter how big the File Manager window is, so long as you can see some of the Program Manager window behind it. Go to the directory where your files are located.

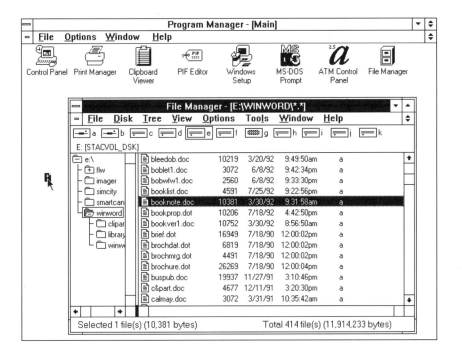

5
Now drag a file icon into Program Manager. Don't worry—the file icon remains in File Manager, but a copy of the file appears in Program Manager, with a larger icon and the DOS file name. You can do this for as many icons (files) as you like, from different directories, or created by different applications. There's an easier way to do this, described later in this section. When you're ready, close File Manager and click on the **Restore** button to make the Main window into a manageable size.

Instant Gratification

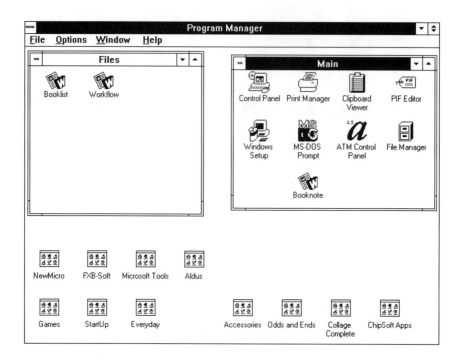

6 Create a Files group in the same way you created the Everyday and Odds and Ends groups in the last section. You can call this **Files,** or **Current Work,** or maybe the name of some client, course title, or other area of responsibility. You can create several group windows, but it's probably better to start with one. You can always add or rename group windows later.

Instant Gratification

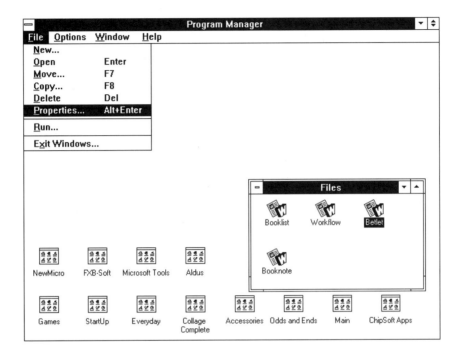

7

Here's the second part of making file icons—giving them
long names. Whenever you deal with them inside programs, they'll have their DOS names, but on the Program
Manager desktop you can call them what you like. The
first step is to highlight the icon—click on it once. Then
go to Program Manager's File menu, and choose **Properties.**

35

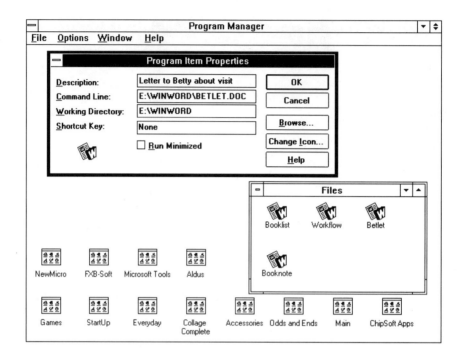

8 The Program Item Properties dialog box has a section called **Description.** This is where you enter the new name for the icon. This changes what appears under the icon. Change the DOS file name to any descriptive name you want. Leave all of the other entries alone—they are what DOS and Windows use to find the file. Notice the Change Icon button and the Run Minimized box—they figure in later exercises.

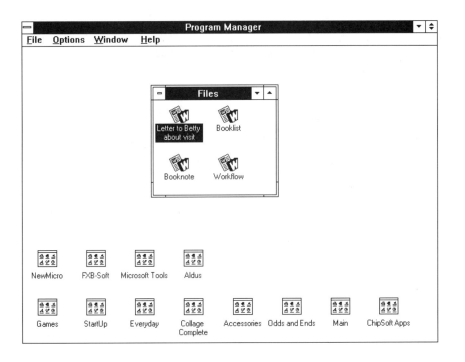

9 Now you can double-click on this icon, and as promised the application starts and the file opens. Your icon has a long description, which will be enough to easily identify it. So why shouldn't you convert all your files to icons like this? If you do you'll clutter up the desktop with dozens of rarely used icons. Stick to the work that's really current. When the file is no longer current, you can delete the icon from Program Manager: You won't be deleting the file.

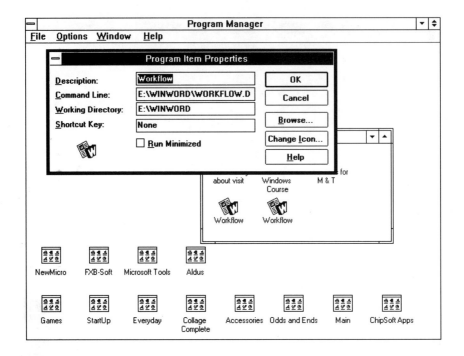

10 There is an easier way to create new file icons, rather than dragging them out of File Manager. If you understand the idea of a DOS file path, this is no problem. Just hold down **Control,** and drag any file icon. This duplicates the icon. However, you need to change the description (as in step nine). With the new icon highlighted, go to the Program Item Properties dialog box as before.

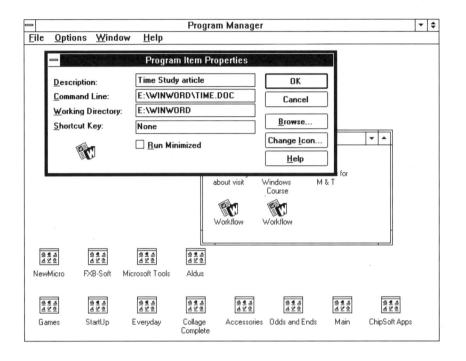

11 Now enter a description of the new file in **Description.** After you've done this, go to the next box, called **Command Line.** If the file is associated, just enter the drive, directory, any subdirectory, and the file name. If you're making a file icon for another file from the same directory, all you need to do is change the name of the file. If the file isn't associated with an application, you'll need to enter the path to the executable file (the .EXE file), followed by one space, and the name of the data file. If the data file isn't in the same file as the executable file, you'll need to enter its full path. Make the Working Directory the same as the directory that holds the executable file.

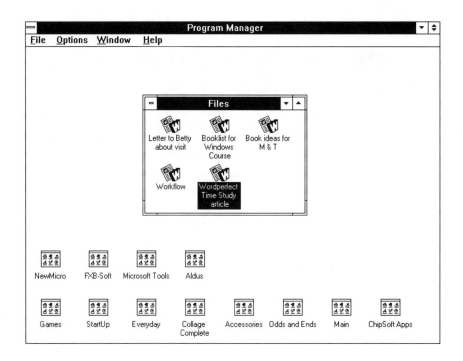

12 You now have an icon that will allow you to double-click on it to start an application and open the data file. However, say the icon design is wrong for the application. Perhaps you want a way of identifying file icons, not by the application that created them, but by an icon that would identify them by client, course of study, or other area. Whatever your reason, you want to change the icon.

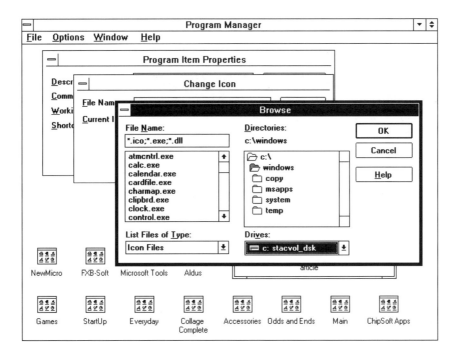

13 In the Program Item Properties dialog box, choose the **Change Icon** button. This shows you all the icons that are available for the application (program) linked to that icon; there are often alternate icons here. If you need an icon for a specific application, click on the **Browse** button and find the .EXE file that runs the application.

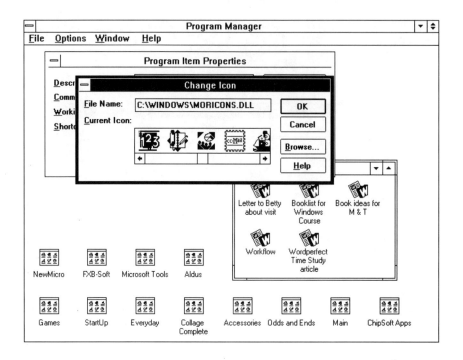

14 If you just want a different icon, look in the Windows directory at PROGMAN.EXE and MORICONS.DLL. There are dozens of icons here, some are specific to an application, but plenty are general-purpose designs. Whatever you choose, click on an icon, choose **OK** in the dialog box, and your file will have a new icon.

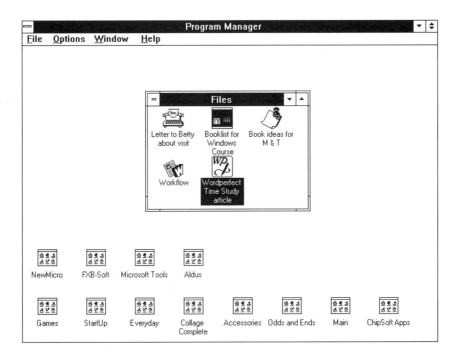

15 Here's a new icon for the file, along with icons from PROGMAN.EXE and MORICONS.DLL. The Program Item Properties dialog box lets you change just about anything an icon can do. For instance, you can even make a Word for Windows icon start up Excel. Of course, being a nice person, you'd never do that to someone else's machine. Pity.

Instant Gratification

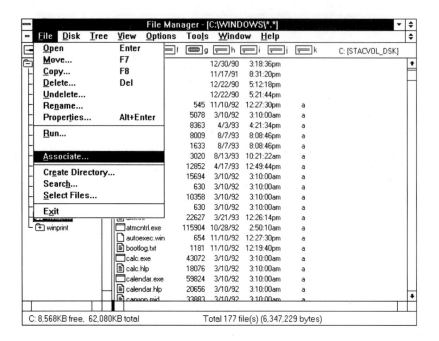

16 You can associate (link) any type of file with any program; the only restriction is that an extension can only be associated with one application. But applications can have many extensions associated with them. Associations are normally set up when you install the program, but you can add to or change these. You need to be in File Manager, and select **Associate** from the File Menu. Enter an extension in the **Files with Extension** box. Then either choose an application from the **Associate With box,** or find an executable file (an .EXE file) by clicking on **Browse.**

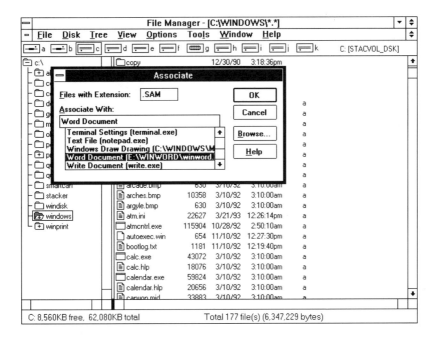

17 Although WordPerfect and Ami Pro are not installed on this computer, it's possible that you may want to use files created by them—if someone brings you a floppy, for instance. So .WP5 and .SAM files are associated with Word for Windows, and will open it automatically. You still have to tell Word that these are WordPerfect or Ami files, but the process is much faster than going through Word's File Open dialog box.

Instant Gratification

45

Instant Gratification

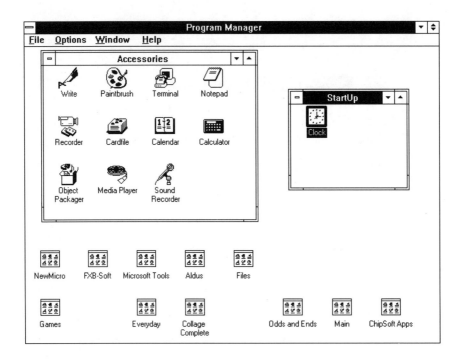

18 Here's a useful way to tell the time and date—use the Windows Clock. Open the Accessories group, and double-click on the clock icon There's a way to have Clock open at the start of every Windows session, and for it to be visible in every application. This is where you use the **Windows StartUp** group, and we'll be taking further advantage of StartUp later. For now, drag the **Clock** icon into the StartUp group.

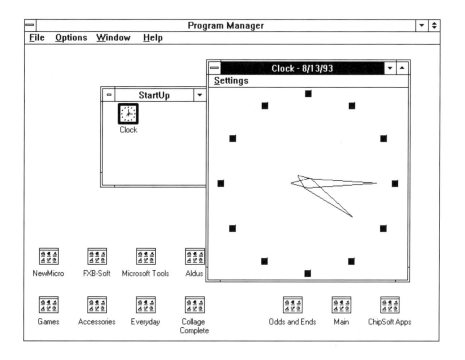

19 With Clock in the StartUp group, it will run every time
you start Windows. Of course, it will only be visible in
Program Manager, and may obscure something important,
so you'll need to change it to a better size and position.
Clock has two important menus; Settings, which is in the
usual place, and an extra item at the bottom of the
Control menu. (You can usually ignore the Control menu;
it's the menu that drops down from the button in the top
left of your application.)

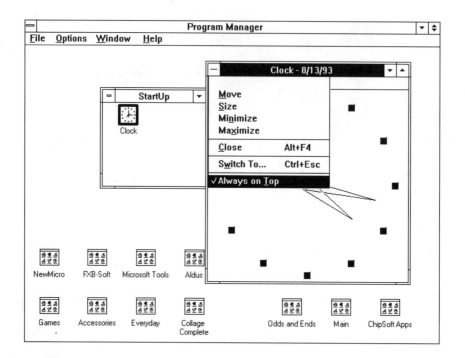

20 This is the Control menu item that affects Clock and it's the only application that has it. Selecting **Always on Top** will ensure that the clock stays in front of any application that you run. Applications run on top of Program Manager (or in front of Program Manager—the two terms are interchangeable). This means that the clock will be visible in Program Manager and visible when you start another application.

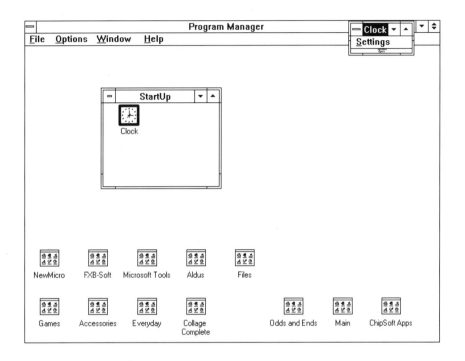

21 The Clock window needn't be very big to be useful, but it's easier to see the time when the readout is digital. I like to have seconds showing, along with the date. Drag the corners of the Clock window to make it about one and a half inches wide by a little over half an inch high. Don't worry that you can't see the time for the menu bar. Move the icon to the top right of your screen, so that it's just to the left of the Minimize button.

49

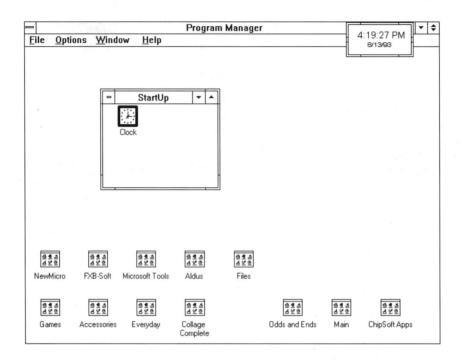

22 Now open the settings menu and select **No Title.** The menu bar disappears, leaving just the time and the date. If you want to get the menu bar back, double-click anywhere in the window. The time and date that you see are those set by the system however they don't always keep good time. Go to the Control Panel (in Program Manager's Main window) and select **Date/Time** to correct any inaccuracy.

Instant Gratification

3

Using Windows Multitasking

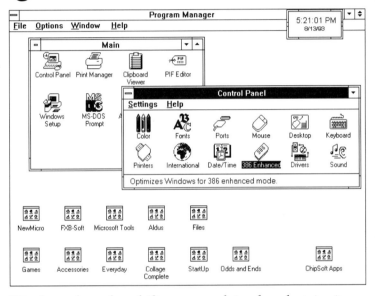

 Windows has the ability to multitask—that is, it can do more than one thing at a time. Although only one person uses a computer at any given time, there are still many ways of exploiting this. You may not have sufficient RAM to run more than one program, so you'll have to take advantage of Windows virtual memory. This means that Windows treats some of the hard drive as extra RAM; this slows programs down, but as a rule you'll only be using one application at a time. To set up virtual memory, choose **Control Panel** from Program Manager's Main window.

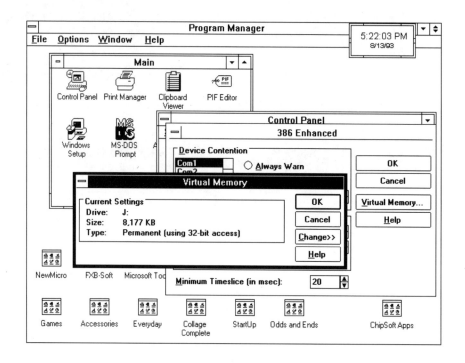

2 When you choose **386 Enhanced**, you get a dialog box. Don't worry about the settings in the 386 Enhanced dialog box, leave them as they are. To set up virtual memory by creating a swap file, you'll need to click the **Virtual Memory** button. That sends you to the Virtual Memory dialog box. Unless you're short of uncompressed hard disk space, you should consider setting up eight megabytes of virtual memory. Your dialog box may show that you have more than this, less than this, or no virtual memory at all. Unless your virtual memory is around eight megabytes, and Permanent (using 32-bit access) you should change it. Click the **Change** button.

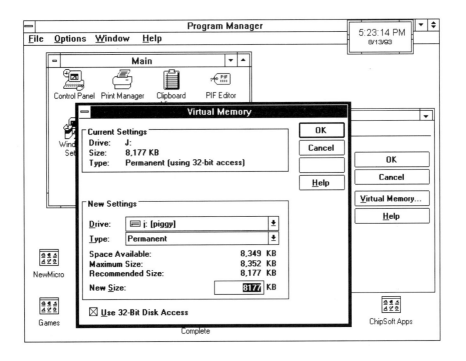

3 You may already have a huge swap file. They are sometimes set up on new computers, when the hard drives are almost empty. Enter **8192** in the **New Size** box. You should see the **Use 32-bit Disk Access** box below this. If this is not grayed out, make sure the box has an **X** in it. This will speed your disk accesses, but some disk controllers (particularly on portables) can't deal with it. Select **OK,** and then choose **OK** in subsequent dialog boxes to get you back to Control Panel. If you created a brand-new swap file, you'll find that your hard drive now has eight megabytes less space and a hidden file called 386SPART.PAR.

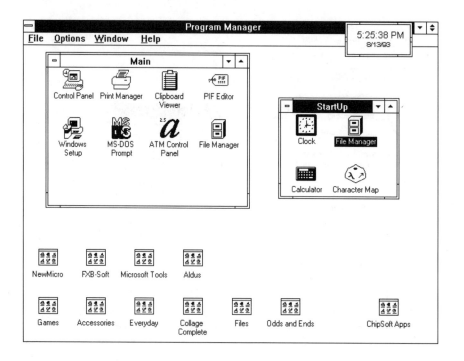

4 Now that you've created virtual memory, how are you going to use it? The best way to take advantage of virtual memory is to have several applications running at once. Probably only one will be doing anything at any one time, but you won't have to stop one application and start another. To get applications running as soon as you start your Windows session, move or copy their icons into the StartUp group window. I have Clock, Character Map, and Calculator from the Accessories group. This is as good a time as any to drag that copy of the File Manager icon out of the Everyday group and into StartUp.

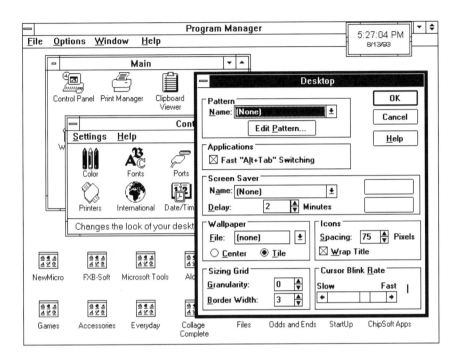

5 You still need to do some setting up to make multitasking run smoothly—you may even have to tell Windows that you need to use Multitasking, although this is normally set up when you install Windows. Check it by going to the Control Panel, from Program Manager's Main group. Choose the **Desktop** icon and look for the Applications box. If it isn't checked, make sure there's an **X** in **Fast "Alt+Tab" Switching.** The folks at Microsoft were so pleased with this that they called it the *Cool Switch.* When you see what it can do for you, you'll probably agree.

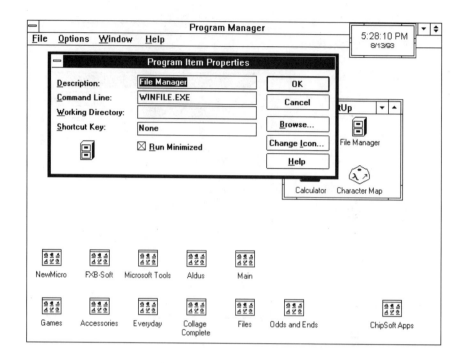

6 If you started Windows now, what would happen? Clock, Character Map, Calculator and File Manager would all open over Program Manager. You want all of them, except Clock, to run as icons; when you use the *Cool Switch* (**Alt+Tab**) they'll open to full size. Select each icon (except Clock) individually, and choose **Properties** in Program Manager's File menu. Check the **Run Minimized** box to make sure that they don't get in the way.

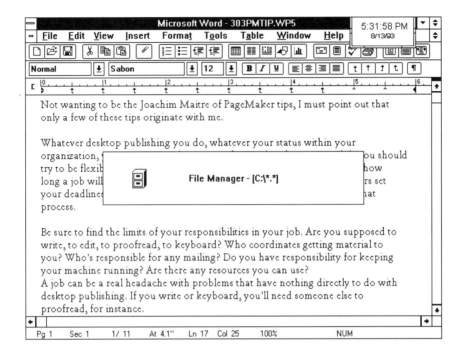

7 Now you're set to use multitasking. Suppose you're in Word for Windows, and you realize that you'll need to save your work to a diskette. Without multitasking, you'd have to quit Word for Windows and open File Manager to format the diskette. Further, suppose you need the file in the WordPerfect format. You'll have to reopen Word for Windows and do a **Save As** in WordPerfect format. With multitasking, you hold down the **Alt** key and briefly press on **Tab.** In the center of your screen, you'll see a window that shows another application. If this is the one you want, let go of the **Alt** key. If not, press **Tab** again until you get the application you want.

57

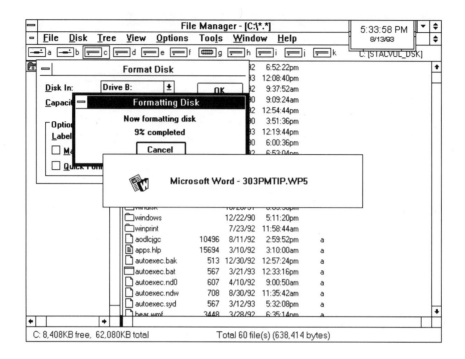

8 Now do whatever you want in the application, but when you're done, don't **Exit.** Just press **Alt** and **Tab** in the same way until you see the icon for the application you were in, and release the **Alt** Key. You'll be back in the program at exactly the same place as before. You can **Alt+Tab** out of an application with a dialog box open; you can Alt+Tab out of File Manager while it's formatting a diskette, however other applications will not run as fast as normal until the formatting is done.

Instant Gratification

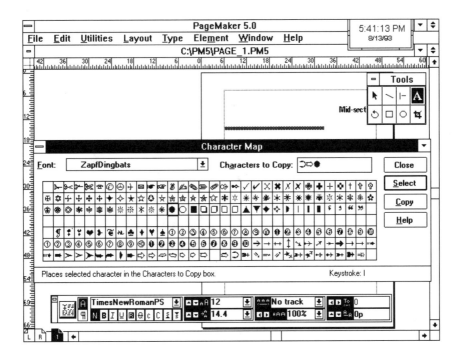

9

Another application that is useful to have handy is **Character Map.** You may want to add a special character to a document; one of the Windows characters that you can't see on the keyboard, or a character from a font like Symbol or Dingbats. This normally means that you have to look something up on a chart, however Windows provides that chart for you in Character Map. You can copy and paste the character into your document and then hide Character Map until the next time you need it.

Instant Gratification

59

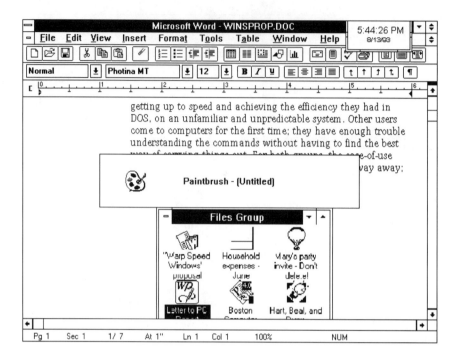

10 Suppose you're in a word processor, and you need a simple illustration. **Minimize** the word processor, and open **Paintbrush** from Program Manager. Create the illustration, save it, but don't exit Paintbrush. **Alt+Tab** your way back to the word processor, and import the illustration by selecting **Copy** in the edit menu of Paintbrush. Then in the word processor, use the **Paste** feature. Maybe it isn't quite right; **Alt+Tab** back into Paintbrush, open the illustration if necessary, and alter and save it. Now **Alt+Tab** back to the word processor and import the illustration again.

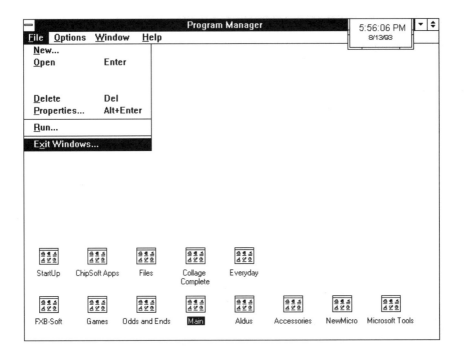

11 You may lose track of all the applications you've opened. No problem! **Alt+Tab** to Program Manager when you want to end your session, and then choose Exit Windows. You'll see *Do you want to save changes messages* for every application that has an open file.

Instant Gratification

Section Two

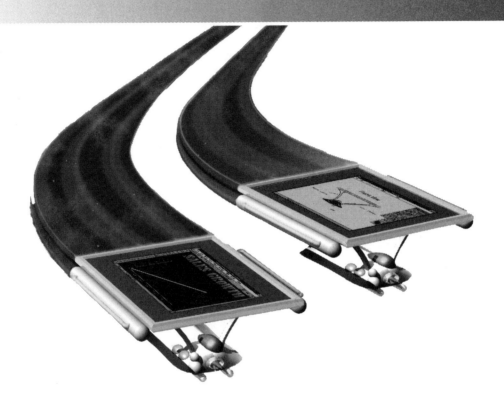

For People who read instructions

4

Hardware

It may seem unusual to start off with a discussion of hardware. However, the main thrust of this book is that it's not what computer you have, but how you use it. Machine power plays some part in productivity, but not as much as you think. Since, you have to buy some computer, you might as well get the best you can. In the first part of this chapter I'll talk about the different features of computers. In the second, I'll describe how these features affect speed and whether or not you need them.

Today's PC is collection of interrelated pieces. Therefore, a single fast component won't necessarily make a vast difference, while one slow component can slow down the rest of the machine. You need to make sure that every part of the computer is running efficiently. If you're buying a new computer, you need to specifically chose each component so that nothing slows you down.

Who's who in the market

Although companies like IBM and Compaq sell the most PCs, they don't dominate the market. IBM, currently the largest seller, has only around 12 percent of the market. The total market share of the top ten manufacturers is approximately 40 percent; the remaining 60 percent of the market belongs to hundreds of smaller companies.

Consequently, there are very few computer manufacturers. There are, however, plenty of computer assemblers who take several major components and put them together. However few companies create any major part of the computer. IBM, Compaq, and Dell are some of the members of this very small group—most advance and change comes from a small number of component manufacturers who sell the same product to all buyers.

Since the products of component manufacturers must be accepted by the technically adept staff of computer assemblers (rather than naive end-users), the quality of components is high. There is always another manufacturer with a similar product waiting to steal away customers.

You, too, can be a computer manufacturer. Just buy motherboards with all the circuitry installed, get cases and power supplies, add floppy and hard drives, video boards, and monitors. Since nearly any component will work with any other, you may choose where to draw the line between power and price. Further, you can switch suppliers any time you need more components; all you need is a nameplate for identification and a plan to sell your computers.

Why Computers Run Fast or Slow

Computers run fast or slow for many reasons, design, sufficient resources, and incompatibility are just a few. The major parts of the computer that can affect overall speed are:

- CPU chips
- Circuit board design
- Video cards
- Cache memory

Parts that affect the speed if they aren't sufficiently large:

- RAM memory
- Free space on the hard disk

The following parts affect the speed, but don't vary greatly from machine to machine:

- Hard disk drives
- Floppy disk drives

Parts that don't affect the speed at all, unless they are badly designed or not up to current standards, are:

- The keyboard
- The mouse
- The monitor

If you run a Windows computer, the odds are that your CPU (or chip) was made by Intel. If not, it works in a similar manner and its power is referenced to a similar Intel chip. Therefore the discussion about Intel chips applies to the products of other companies' as well.

Intel made the chip that powered the first PCs over ten years ago, but these chips can't run Windows 3.1. The lowest powered chips that can are the 80286 series (the 286) and they can't use Windows' virtual memory (I'll explain what virtual memory is later in the book). However, 80286 computers haven't been sold widely for some years and the other components of this computer probably wouldn't be up to present-day standards. If you can afford it, switch to something more modern.

Which Chip Is Which?

The major Intel chips are the 80386 series (the 386), the 80486 series (the 486), and the Pentium. All of these can run all the features of Windows 3.1. The 386 was the successor to the 286; the 486 followed the 386; and finally, the Pentium is Intel's latest CPU. All these chips come with different clock speeds. Each chip family has better performance than its predecessors, which makes the computer run faster. In addition, faster clock speeds within the family of chips makes the CPU speedier.

Why is the power of the CPU important? Because the CPU not only does all the math, it organizes the rest of the computer's components. A computer with a faster chip will do every action faster, even if all the other components are the same. So it makes sense to get the fastest CPU that you can afford.

Computers No, Data Processing Yes

The word computer is a misleading term—it implies that the main function of the machine is mathematics. This may have been true when computers filled a room and were tended by people in white coats, but the more modern term *data processing* best describes the way computers are used now.

Suppose you use the search feature to look for a word in a document you've written. The document is stored as groups of numbers. The program then takes the characters you're looking for and also converts them to numbers. The program then subtracts each word from the search word. If the answer is zero, then the words must be the same. While there are other processes going on, the only math in this exercise is subtraction.

Moving words in and out of the CPU from memory is more complex. The screen must simultaneously display the area of the document where a match occurs and show a dialog box asking if you want to continue. Eventually, the whole process must come to a halt when every word has been examined. In other words, the CPU performs a few thousand subtractions, but spends far more time moving data around in memory and on the screen. The actual data doesn't change; hence the term data processing. In addition to performing mathematical processing, the CPU must also move data around and control the other components in the computer.

Another variation in CPU specifications is the presence or absence of a math co-processor. This only works on numbers the chip can't hold in memory as normal numbers (which are called integers). Rather, the numbers are so vast that a figure like five billion must be stored in the form of 5×10^9 (called floating point). It isn't important that you understand this, just be aware that the computer can store numbers up to two billion without needing a math coprocessor. In earlier CPUs, the math coprocessor was a separate chip that could increase processing speed of floating point numbers hundreds of times. In the 386, 486, and Pentium chips, the coprocessor is part of the chip. However, some 386 and 486 CPUs don't have a coprocessor and are called 386SX and 486SX.

What's On the Motherboard?

Computer assemblers usually buy their CPUs on motherboards. Mother boards are circuit boards about a foot square that hold all the chips which make up the computer. There are just a few companies making these motherboards, and performance varies slightly between them. However, the differences are so slight that it's unlikely you'll need to choose one computer over another on the basis of the motherboard.

One type of motherboard design widely used is the local bus. Instead of using the data pathway that services much of the rest of the PC (known as the AT bus), local bus connects the processor directly with video circuitry, the hard drive controller, and other peripherals. Local bus operates at the speed of the processor, which can be three to five times faster than the AT bus and moves data in segments four times larger. The theory is that the AT bus is a bottleneck in today's computers with fast CPUs, moving large amounts of data.

EISA bus motherboards have been used for several years because they have a data path as large as local bus. However, the bus speed is the same as the AT bus. EISA is found in computers where large amounts of data have to be transferred, like the computers that hold databases and supply this data to other computers on a network.

Why Video Cards Are Important

The component with the widest speed range is the video card. The video card can be unaccelerated, or have a video acccelerator chip that lets it process images 50 times faster than standard. The average computer only uses the video circuitry approximately 12 percent of the time; so even a major increase in speed won't be very noticeable.

Video cards also control the number of colors your monitor can display and set the resolution (or sharpness) of the image. They decide a very important specification—the image refresh rate. The image is constantly redrawn on the screen, many times a second. If this refresh rate is around 60 times a second or lower, the screen will flicker and make long work sessions difficult. A few monitors cannot sustain the high refresh rates of 70 times a second or greater which provide a steady image.

Video accelerators work by taking the video processing workload off the CPU and transferring it to a specialized chip that is optimized for display work. Many accelerators only work with Windows' graphics commands, but some will work with both DOS and Windows programs.

Cache Memory—Enough Will Do

Cache Memory speeds up processing by putting needed information in the Type Memory where it can be reached fastest. Imagine that you are working at a small desk in a library and need information from the volumes on the shelves. You may begin by going to the shelves, bringing the book to your desk, getting the information, and then returning the volume to the shelf.

After a while, you may notice that you're taking information from the same book several times, so the next time you keep the volume on your desk. You may also find this happens with other books, so eventually you have several on your desk. If you continue to do this, eventually you'll have no room on your desk for any more books. At this point you must decide which book would be the best one to return to the shelves in order to make room on your desk. You'll probably choose the one you haven't looked at recently.

This is the way a cache works. Without a cache, the computer takes information from a file (as you did with a book) and then discards it. With a cache, the computer keeps the file in a form of memory that's easy to access (as you did by putting the book on your desk). Eventually, the memory is filled, and the computer deletes a file from the cache to make room for new files (as you did when you put a book back on the shelf). The file still exists in a slower form of memory, just as the book still exists—it is merely in a less convenient location.

71

The hit and miss world of caches

Computers are not as smart as people While you may know that one book is going to be useful, the computer has no way of understanding to which file it might return. Consequently, the computer caches all of them. It also keeps a record of when it last looked at a file and if it has to delete a file from the cache, it chooses the one least used. If the information the computer needs is in the cache, that's called a cache hit; and if not, that's a cache miss. Similarly to the way you saved time by not having to walk back to the shelves each time you wanted to look in a book, the computer saves time by not looking in a slower form of memory. By keeping a cache in RAM, the computer doesn't have to look for information on the disk, which can take several hundred times longer.

Caches aren't perfect; every file that's brought into a cache starts off as a cache miss. Sometimes a file need only be read once and then is no longer needed. This file will not be removed from the cache until every other file in the cache has been read or discarded. Some programs read from dozens of files, others from just one or two. In spite of these problems, caches are very helpful, For example, Windows' SmartDrive RAM cache has an efficiency of approximately 90 percent cache hits.

This section of the book isn't about SmartDrive and similar RAM caches as these are covered later in the book. This section is concerned with those caches using memory chips purely for this purpose—SmartDrive, on the other hand, is a way of configuring part of your RAM using software. You'll find hardware caches inside and immediately outside the CPU, as well as on disk drives and some disk controllers.

Because today's CPUs are so fast, they need information faster than the main memory can supply it. The solution is to have a cache on the CPU itself, and a larger cache externally. If this cache wasn't present, the CPU would have to wait until the information could be retrieved from RAM. Thus, a cache allows the CPU to carry on processing. A typical 486 machine has an 8K cache built-in to the CPU, and up to 256K externally. The Pentium has two 8K caches and up to 512K externally. The external cache uses memory chips three or four times faster than normal RAM; unfortunately they're also more expensive. Hard disk drives come with a cache, typically 64K. The electronics on the disk drive control the cache. There is another form of hard disk cache—a part of some hard disk controllers, it has memory similar to RAM and can have several additional megabytes of memory installed.

What's Different About Your Computer? Nothing

Welcome to the wonderful world of computer advertisements, where every manufacturer promises something to make your work fly by; something you can't be without. Each company appears to have made some technological breakthrough which will revolutionize your computing, with *blazing speed* that will *blow away* all competitors.

The truth is that computer assemblers (and that means almost everybody selling computers) offer pretty much the same product. With a few CPU manufacturers, about a dozen hard-disk drive makers, and some thirty companies making monitors, it's highly probable there are fewer PC configurations than there are nameplates. Rapid change in technology means that many advertised systems are already discontinued, or superseded by machines with newer, faster components. It takes just a few months for a new feature to become standard on nearly all assemblers' machines.

In an effort to differentiate one company from another each offers everything their competition does. As a result, there are hordes of "me-too" features listed in the ads. In addition, numerous comparison charts show the latest technology as a vast improvement over older machines, and usually over the competition's machines as well.

73

Whether or not you buy from one of the companies that advertise in magazines, you'll probably shop for the same list of features at a local dealer or superstore. Whatever your level of knowledge about computers, most sales people will reel off all the speed features each computer has to offer.

The Need for Speed

The obvious question to ask yourself is *How much speed do I need*? This is often confused with the question *How much speed do I want*! You'll need to be honest with yourself as there isn't a simple answer. You should first look to what you expect to do with the machine.

You may intend to buy a computer because you want to see what they are all about, or you think it would be good for your kids to have one. You may have simple needs: writing letters, basic accounting for home or a small business, keeping expense records, and similar tasks. If this is all you will do on your computer nearly any one will do—in the beginning.

Most people want to run more complex programs. They want to use their computer for general office work, or work they bring home. These people know that they need more power than a basic machine provides, but usually guess at what to buy. Such buyers generally end up with something in the midrange. Often they decide to spend the previous amount each time they replace a computer ($2,000 for example) and rely on improvements in technology to give them a needed boost.

Finally, there are the power users—real and imagined. Some run photomanipulation software, want a file server for a network, or have a very complex spreadsheet or database. For these people, any increase in power translates into extra production. There are a number of users who use their job status or interest in computers to get the latest and greatest on their desk, whether they need it or not.

How Long Will You Run This Computer?

Once you have decided which group you fit into the next decision is more complex: *How long do you intend to keep the computer?* and *What do you intend to do with it? If your needs change, will you buy another machine?*

The average business computer is changed every three years; the average home machine every five. If you buy a computer more powerful than you currently need, you'll be ready if you take on more demanding work. The useful life of the computer will be longer. Alternatively, if you don't foresee any changes, you'll waste money on a powerful machine. If you envisage buying a new machine should your needs change, then it pays to buy just enough computer for what you need now.

This process is complicated because software changes so often that no one can predict what will be an adequate machine in a few years. Two or three years ago, photomanipulation programs were unknown on the PC; now such a program is merely one module of a $99 multi-program graphics software bundle. Other technologies, such as virtual reality and desktop video, are applications that require powerful computers in order to run.

You may need more computer than you think

Even if your tastes don't run to the exotic, you may regret not buying enough computer. When Windows was introduced, its RAM requirements (four megabytes) seemed excessive by the standards of the typical computer of 1990. But this is now commonplace and most DOS applications are no longer being improved. If you refused to upgrade your machine and stayed with DOS you may wish you'd made the change.

Most people take a guess and buy more than they need in the hope that the computer will stay current for its intended life. The three year cycle of business machines is easier to justify since last year's power-user machines become this year's hand-me-downs to the next level. The 286 machines at the bottom of the heap are often donated to charity or sold to employees.

If you intend to keep your home computer for at least five years it's advisable to buy all the programs for your current needs and stay away from computer magazines. Some people buy a home machine intending to learn a computer-based skill like desktop publishing and hope to be self-employed some day. If this is your aim then you can start with a basic machine and upgrade as soon as you go into business for yourself.

Now that you've defined some of your requirements, it's time to take a look at what's available.

Choosing the Dream Machine

Although a 286 machine will satisfy your needs for basic applications, it's not a good buy. It will have to be bought used, as 286s haven't been sold new for some time. As a result, the other components—disk drive, video card, and memory—won't run Windows well—if at all. Upgrading a 286 is not cost-effective. To do so you'd have to replace almost all the important components and by that time it would cost you nearly as much as the price of a brand new 386 or even 486. Also, the parts replaced wouldn't be easy to sell, or for that matter, nor would the computer.

A 386 is a much better investment. A 386 will have enough memory in it without having to use special memory cards and the video circuits and hard disk are probably passable. If they are not, an upgrade is simple. The 386 runs Windows in enhanced mode, that is, it lets you run several programs at once. There are still a few new 386s of this type in the stores, but most will be used.

Buying a new computer

The choice in new machines is between a 486 and a Pentium. If you're not sure whether you need a Pentium machine, you probably don't. If a Pentium machine sells for less than $750 over the cost of an equivalent 486, then it's worth considering. 486 computers have an excellent price performance ratio; the fastest machines sell for little more than the slower machines. If you're looking for a computer that won't run out of performance, a fast 486 is an excellent choice.

However, if saving money is an issue, any 486 will do for most work. A 486 is faster than the 386 and costs little more than $1,000 (which is about the lowest price you should expect to pay for a complete computer). You might be offered a 486SX-25, which identifies a 486 chip running at 25 Mhz and doesn't have a co-processor (the version of the CPU chip with the co-processor is called the DX). For this price you should expect four Megabytes of RAM, and at least 170 Megabytes of hard disk space. This will be enough to run several Windows applications.

The top of the 486 line is the 486-66, though faster versions will be available soon. These computers have features that may not be offered in the lower-priced models. These features include local bus video, accelerated video cards, larger monitors with better resolution, and local bus disk controllers. Some models offer the EISA data bus and caching hard drive controllers. Ask yourself what features are worth paying for.

How to rate them

The computer's clock speed is the most important feature. Even if all the other components are the same, a 486-66 will run almost twice as fast as a 486-25 on typical business applications. On tests of the processor alone, the difference will be greater—but the work you do involves all sections of the computer.

The 486-66 is a DX2 chip. This chip runs at 66 Mhz internally and 33 Mhz externally. As a result whenever the processor needs to get information from RAM, it must communicate at half speed. Is this a problem? The 486-50DX2 chip computes at around 95 percent of the rate of the 486-50DX chip that runs at the same speed inside and out. Much of this is due to the cache memory inside the chip, which still runs at high speed. Since circuit boards are more difficult to design when information moves around at high speeds, a DX2 chip computer is cheaper.

Processor benchmarks will also show up the 486SX-25's lack of a math coprocessor. As with the 386, cheaper models of the chips don't have a coprocessor. The circuitry exists, but it's disabled. Sometimes there's an error in the coprocessor circuitry, but the main reason for disabling the coprocessor circuitry is so that Intel can offer CPU chips in a range of prices.

The obvious question is *Do you need a coprocessor?* The answer is usually no, because so few programs use them. Most programs function very well within a number limit of two billion. If the numbers exceed this, programs automatically store them as floating-point and just take longer to deal with them. Certain programs in particular situations will take longer to run without a coprocessor, but word processing, database, and many other programs never need them. If you have the choice between an SX and a DX version of the same CPU speed machine, take the savings on the SX model.

Why you don't need a large cache

The next element is the external CPU cache. Sometimes this is 128K, sometimes 256K. If the information is not in the cache, the computer spends three times as long retrieving it from the main RAM. This cache is in addition to the 8K cache inside the CPU itself. Tests have shown that any external cache provide little improvement in CPU speed; after 64K, improvements are negligible.

The truth about caches is that even a tiny cache is a vast improvement over no cache, but increasing the size of the cache makes little difference. This is because there are very few large files on most computers. My machine has over 6,000 files, yet only 16 are larger than a Megabyte. Including these files, there are only about a hundred over 256K, which consists of less than two percent of total files. Most of the large files are program and help files which will be read into RAM once during a session. The average file size is under 50K.

RAM—not enough will slow you down

The next element is the main RAM. You can seriously cripple Windows by running it with insufficient memory. In this situation, Windows uses part of the hard drive as virtual memory—in effect treating it as RAM. This is useful when you're trying to run several programs at once, but if this is necessary merely to run Windows and one or two applications, you're in trouble.

This solution is undesirable because Windows consists of many small programs called Dynamic Link Libraries, or DLLs—which Windows applications use in order to run. While DOS helps DOS programs communicate with the computer, DLLs are part of Windows applications. This is the reason why Windows applications look and act the same; they are the same, because you're seeing the DLLs in action. Dialog boxes, the menu bar, and running the cut and paste function are all parts of Windows, not the program which displays them.

If you have insufficient RAM, the DLL files have to be located on the hard drive. Access time is several hundred times slower than if they were in RAM and this slowdown happens many times when you're running a program. Although it's possible to run Windows with under two megabytes of RAM, everything will process very slowly. With two megabytes of RAM installed you can run a single program, but there will still be diminished performance. The recommended RAM is four megabytes, and unless individual programs require more, this will be sufficient.

There's no benefit to adding RAM that is rated faster than the RAM that's already installed. However, you can cause problems by adding memory that's slower. If you're not certain of this, or any other technical work, local companies that repair computers will fit the correct components. My local CompUSA charges $30 to add RAM, and $50 to add a hard disk.

There are very slight differences in the way circuit boards are designed. Otherwise identical computers can perform differently because of this. However, you'll only notice the differences with benchmark testing, and it's not worth choosing a computer because of the make of motherboard.

Hard Drives—knowing what counts

Hard drives come in a range of standards. The common types are ISA standard IDE interface, local bus IDE, EISA IDE, and SCSI. All the options to ISA IDE improve the speed of data transfer. This is noticeable only when they're dealing with large files, which are rare on the average computer. If you're running a file server—the computer that's the *boss* of a network—then one of the other types are worth considering. Otherwise, stick with ISA or local bus IDE. A new version of SCSI called SCSI-2 may speed up transferring smaller files.

How long should you have to wait for a hard drive? You can find out by opening a large program and then accessing the Help function. This will be a cache miss, because the cache has no way of knowing that you're going to need the file until you ask for it. On my 486-66, it took Word for Windows around two seconds to open its help file, which is nearly two Megabytes. Not all of this time is taken in retrieving the file, and this size file is not going to be accessed regularly. Therefore, I can't see that increasing disk speed would have an appreciable effect on the way I work.

80

Average access time is another disk drive specification. Although this affects all disk drive reads and writes, a disk cache like SmartDrive will even out just about every difference between drives. Some manufacturers offer hard disk controllers with memory so that you can use it as a cache. In the very rare instances, where you can't use a cache in RAM, this might be useful; it's cheaper to add RAM if necessary. Disk controller caches don't supplement RAM caches—in fact, it's usually necessary to turn off SmartDrive to get the best from controller caches.

Why your TEMP directory is important

One underestimated specification is the amount of free space on your hard drive. If you are within a megabyte or two of full disk capacity then you should consider offloading some files. The reason for this is that while all your directories remain a constant size through each Windows session, there's one that grows while you run an application and then returns to its normal size. This is your TEMP directory, and it's where various applications place their temporary files.

When you exit from an application, the application deletes its temporary files (they will have the suffix .TMP), and so you're not aware that the disk space has been used. The only time you'll notice that the directory is being used is when you have a system crash and have to restart your computer. In this case, the temporary files remain in the directory and may be crucial if you lose work. To find seemingly lost files, look in your TEMP directory, and sort the files by date. If there's a file with a date and time close to the time of the crash, rename it with the correct suffix for the program you were running (.DOC for Word for Windows, for instance), and then try to open it within the program.

Some applications leave files in the TEMP directory and don't delete them. Often there are files left from when you installed programs. Take a look at the files in your TEMP directory. If no applications are running, you can safely delete any files you find there. The location of your TEMP directory may be specified in your AUTOEXEC.BAT file (SET TEMP = C:\TEMP, for example); if not, then Windows uses the DOS directory for temporary files.

A significant problem occurs when you have a small amount of free space for temporary files. This is due to the fact that programs have to adjust their use of your free disk space and may not be able to open large files or install new programs because there is simply no space available for a large temporary file. If your C drive is almost full and your hard disk is portioned into C and D drives, you could change your AUTOEXEC.BAT file to read SET TEMP = D:\TEMP. You must then create a TEMP directory on your D drive to make this work.

The other kind of disk drive is the floppy, since both sizes of floppy disks are still commonplace it's not worthwhile to get a computer with only one size of drive. Floppy drives are very slow; the average access time is at least ten times that of a hard drive. You can't change this, but you can avoid using floppy drives as much as possible. Floppy disks should be used purely for backing up your work (although a tape drive is better) or for transporting data. Never open a program and start reading from a floppy disk; always copy the data to your hard drive.

Video—Local Bus, VESA, and other terms you should know

The area that has seen the biggest improvement is in video. Windows places far more demands than DOS on the video circuitry, and this has led to Local Bus and accelerated video cards. The theory is fine, but in practice the improvements are not quite what you'd expect.

Local bus helps complex video instructions to move quickly from the CPU to the video adapter, and with an unaccelerated card the improvements can be very noticeable—maybe twice the normal. As you accelerate the video card, you find that the advantages of local bus decline to around a thirty or forty percent increase.

The reason for this is in the way in which accelerated video cards work. If there is no acceleration, the CPU does most of the processing, and sends a large amount of information to the video card. If the data path between the CPU and the video card is narrow, then the information doesn't come fast enough for the video card and the screen redraws more slowly.

Accelerated video cards do much of the processing that the CPU used to do, so they don't require the detailed information that a non-accelerated card does. As a result, there's much less data traveling from the CPU to the video card, and the data path between the two is less critical.

Since they are optimized for just a few video commands, and because they free the CPU for other tasks, accelerated video cards can have a significant effect on video speeds. As much as a thirty-fold increase in speed may occur, but of course this is only on the video parts of the program. However, faster screen redraws are more readily noticeable than faster disk accesses, so an accelerated video card computer feels faster.

Colors, Resolution, *and* Speed

The development of video cards continues. Today's cards have not yet reached the potential state of the art. Intel's new PLI bus will probably continue to improve. An accelerated video card is not expensive, so if you have a VESA local bus machine you can expect to see attractive upgrades for some time to come. Incidentally, video card manufacturers (and the computer companies that use their cards) can give a misleading impression of the capabilities of their cards. They may promise lots of colors, display at a high resolution, and non-flickering monitors, but many of them can't do all three at the same time.

Most Windows applications will run quite successfully on sixteen colors at 640 x 480 resolution. If your video card supports more colors or higher resolution the video speed will be slower. You may find that you need extra colors in graphics applications, and don't want to change video settings (and consequently have to restart Windows) each time. You may also like the broader view that 800 x 600 or 1024 x 768 resolution gives, and don't mind the small performance loss that accompanies higher resolution.

Although it's not strictly a speed-related component, the monitor may affect the amount of useful work you can do. If the quality is not good enough, you'll find that you need to take breaks from the computer. If you have a monitor of 15 inches or greater, it will probably be acceptable, but 14 inch monitors (usually from the bigger computer manufacturers on their lower-cost models) are not as good as they could be. You need a dot pitch of .31 or below, a refresh rate of 70 Hz, and a non-interlaced monitor. In most cases, this is around 50 dollars more than the cheapest monitor. If the monitor you're considering buying isn't fully specified, ask. Be prepared to pay a little extra. Your eyes, as they say, will thank you.

Summary

To summarize, then:

- Buy the fastest processor you can afford
- Buy a DX chip over an SX chip only if you're doing graphics or complex spreadsheets
- 128K is an ample processor cache
- Get 4 MB of RAM
- Local bus hard drives, EISA, and SCSI will show little improvement in the future

- Cached hard drives are not cost effective—use SmartDrive instead

- Local bus video shows some improvement

- Accelerated video cards are important, but expect further developments

Software that can slow you down

There are some speed issues connected with software that have tie-ins with hardware. There's the thorny issue of printer drivers and video drivers. These are small programs that make printers and video boards work with Windows, and are usually loaded when you install Windows or change your hardware. Sometimes these programs don't work correctly in certain odd situations, and occasionally the companies find ways of making the hardware work faster.

Video card drivers from some manufacturers are updated almost monthly. Consequently, it could pay you to ask the company if there are new drivers. You may be able to obtain these directly from the company for a small fee, or the company could have uploaded new drivers to one or more of the big bulletin boards such as CompuServe. Some older drivers have been known to cause system crashes.

You may not know that you can slow down Windows by using too many fonts. When you open Windows, the program creates a table to give font information to every application. This is done by reading entries in the WIN.INI file and retrieving data about each font. When you use over fifty fonts, you'll notice that Windows and each application slows down. When you have several hundred fonts, the slow-down is noticeable.

Fortunately there are programs to manage your fonts. The best-known is Ares Software's FontMinder. FontMinder lets you make packages that contain only the fonts you'll need for a particular application. You can compile packages with combinations of TrueType and Adobe Type 1 fonts, as well as have a package that contains all your fonts if you are not certain which fonts you will use.

Keep your disk defragmentized

You may already know about disk defragmentation. In order to put as much information on the disk as possible, your hard drive will sometimes fill an area occupied by a deleted file with part of a larger file. The remainder of the file is placed elsewhere on the hard disk. As a result, the program has to make two disk accesses instead of one to get the entire file, and that means processing slows down.

Fragmentation doesn't pose much of a problem until it happens to a large number of files. Most hard drives are approximately 5 percent fragmented. Modules in programs such as PC Tools and Norton will defragment your drives. Compressed drives must have their own defragmenters so Stacker and other compression programs include them. If you defragment your drives once a month you'll see peak performance.

Check the Turbo button!

This final tip may seem obvious, but I have seen the need for it in many installations. Most PCs have a *Turbo* button on the front of the case, which intentionally slows down the speed of the chip. When the button is pressed in, an indicator lights to show that the PC is working at normal speed, or a digital speed indicator shows the rated speed of the chip.

What is the turbo button used for? Games! Some of the older games run at the speed of the processor. While that may be fine on machines that run at eight or ten megahertz, but on today's machines the space invaders arrive too fast to be shot down. By turning off the Turbo button, the computer will run slow enough to make the game playable. Most games now run at a playable speed, no matter how fast the computer.

Windows' Solitaire has a section that's speed-dependent. If you win a game, the cards cascade down as fast as the computer can display them. I've often found computers running at slow speed, so check yours and your colleagues' machines. Remind yourself, the next time you err, that almost certainly someone, somewhere, is trying to extract speed from a machine with the Turbo switch on

Benchmarks Aren't Always Right

In early 1993, test staff began noticing that certain video cards had a performance rating on Ziff-Davis Magazines' WinBench test suite that didn't appear to tally with their performance in everyday computing. Some journalists, especially InfoWorld's Steve Gibson, looked into this in more detail and discovered astonishing sections of code in the video driver software of some companies, designed to give better figures on the Graphic Winmarks test. These sections had no actual function.

One card's driver reported that a section of the test had been completed when in fact it had never been carried out. Another set up a cache to speed up repeated test instructions. One part of the Winbench test displayed the words "The quick brown fox jumps over the lazy dog;" this was part of a certain company's driver software, which had the affect of speeding up the display. While all of these methods gave a better score on the test, they wouldn't actually speed up applications.

As a result the Graphics Winmarks test was revised and the companies removed the offending sections of their code. This illustrates what video card companies believe, that the public has such faith in benchmarks that they were prepared to write spurious pieces of code to get better results.

How to make a slow computer "faster"

Tests are often designed to mislead. Suppose that company A has a new computer or piece of software designed to compete with company B. Company A tests its new product, and finds that in ten tests it beats company B's product on five and loses on five. Company A therefore claims quite legally that, "in a selection of everyday tasks," their product won every time. However the results occurred because they merely chose the right five tests.

Suppose Company A's product loses on every test but one. In nine tests, the product is a total of five seconds slower, and in the one instance where it was faster it only managed to win by 0.6 seconds. Company A may then just repeat the winning test ten times, and it's product is still the fastest.

Many products are designed to cover a wide range of uses, but are often strong in some areas and weaker in others. If competitors design their product to be strong in areas where the market leader is weakest, then a "comparison" will show the competitor's product in a good light. This is analogous to a car manufacturer stating "Why buy a seven-seat minivan? Our four-seat car takes just as many journeys to move eight people as a van."

A variation of this theme is to run tests comparing performance for areas in which the average user is unfamiliar. EISA machines outperform ISA machines when moving large data files from a hard drive. However, if you don't have many files large enough to benefit from EISA, then it's hard to justify the expense.

My computer's faster than your computer

Comparisons are supposed to test like-with-like, but one computer company ran tests against the competition with their four megabytes of RAM against the competition's machines with two megabytes. The company's computers connected with printers by means of a network, which can yield impressive gains in speed. The two megabyte machines used the serial port, which made them print about four times slower than using the parallel port, the most common method of connecting PCs to printers.

Another comparison was made between two operating systems. One company ran a survey asking which system was the hardest to set up and run, and claimed users said their company's system was a great deal easier to use than the competition's. Although a faulty comparison, this was almost certainly true. The competition's operating system was a new product, and most users were unfamiliar with it. Any operating system is bound to be confusing at first.

It's best to rely on the results of magazine testing, since such comparisons are run by people with no loyalty to a particular product. Magazines take testing more seriously, and many readers find this the most important part of the magazine. Magazines do occasionally get things wrong, but if a product receives good reviews from a number of publications, you can be certain it's a reasonable buy.

Even if a product doesn't rate a best buy, you should evaluate the shortcomings discussed in the magazine You may never use the features that the better products have and find that the best buy isn't necessarily *your* best buy. Your specialized needs may make the winner the wrong one for you. Magazines like to name an "Editor's Choice" for the value of publicity in advertisements. However, sometimes the difference between the best and the worst is minimal.

Anyone for Snake Oil?

Computers are confusing. People try to pick a good piece of hardware or software for reasons that often don't make sense. Advertisers are well aware of these reasons, and have been exploiting them for a long time. In fact, many of the attitudes of buyers are similar to those of buyers in the days of patent remedies. Do any of these attitudes sound like yours?

- *Anything is better than nothing.* A spoonful of snake oil must be better than taking nothing at all. People who believe this will seriously consider any new idea, since if it's being sold it must have some value. They'll buy any new device or software without considering how much use it will be for them.

- *Two is twice as nice.* If it says "take one spoonful a day," then two spoonfuls must be twice as good. If you believe this, you'll add RAM beyond what you need to increase the size of caches that may already work at maximum efficiency.

- *Mix and match.* If you're sick, you go to two doctors, and take both medicines they prescribe. You'll use a RAM cache and a hard drive cache, then wonder why you don't see any improvement when the data is shuffled from one cache to another.

Upgrades That Are Worthwhile

If you already own a computer, you can upgrade it in several ways. If your computer is a few years old you may find it more cost-effective to replace. If you have a 486SX computer, you may buy an Intel upgrade chip, which doubles the speed of the machine. This will cost a few hundred dollars. To upgrade also adds a coprocessor, but this is not likely to speed up most of your work, because few programs benefit from it.

For the same reason, although you can buy coprocessors for 386 chips for under $100, an upgrade isn't worthwhile. 386 machines benefit from a motherboard upgrade, where the entire circuit board is replaced, including the CPU. This can cost as little as six or seven hundred dollars for a 486-66 local bus board. The problem is that this investment is close to the cost of a new computer. It's a lot easier to sell your old computer complete than to try to sell the motherboard. But if cash is tight you may have no other option.

If you don't have four megabytes of RAM, you should seriously consider getting the balance. Even three megabytes of RAM costs around $100 if you shop around, and increasing the total to four megabytes will give you a noticeable boost. Many prefer to give this job to a local repair shop, rather than try to select and fit the correct components themselves.

Hard drive prices have fallen considerably, to approximately one-fifth of their price five years ago. A few Windows applications can easily fill 100 megabytes, and newer hard drives access data three times as fast as a few years ago. A good repair shop can install a second hard drive and make it your C drive, so that the original drive is relegated to long-term storage.

Finally, an accelerated video card will have a major effect on your display, even if you don't have local bus. Local bus video cards are very similar to non-local bus cards. It's likely that improvements in graphics acceleration will be available to everybody. Make certain that your monitor has the capability of refreshing the screen fast enough.

Always remember that upgrading a computer may not be the best solution. If you can sell your old computer and buy a new one for an extra $1,000, this is probably a better solution than spending money on replacing components that you can't easily sell as parts. Also, every part of a computer is constantly being improved, so you may find that parts you never intended to upgrade need to be replaced to keep the computer running at an acceptable speed.

The bottom line on fast

Is there any objective ruling on how much speed you need? Unfortunately there isn't. "Fast enough" is too subjective a standard. It's very easy to move to a faster computer for a while and then find that your old machine is unacceptably slow. Still, there's no denying that any 486 computer is fast when running most basic applications.

Today's CPUs are more than up to the task. We rarely notice the wait while the CPU is operating—in fact, it's usually some other component, like the disk drives, slowing the computer. If we doubled the speed of the CPU we'd probably not get much more work done, although we'd probably be aware that the machine was responding somewhat more quickly. The only area where CPU performance has a noticeable effect on productivity is in areas like complex graphics, where some processes are measured in hours.

I recently worked on a 486-25SX, as opposed to my normal 486-66. Most of the time I wasn't aware of the speed difference, but the work was everyday activities—word processing, and basic desktop publishing.

From this experience, I'd say that a basic 486-25SX will be fine in all applications except where the computer is used for complex work.

As time passes, some of today's complex applications will become common, and the 486-25SX will show its age while the 486-66 will still seem fast enough. There are plenty of 386SX computers that seemed fast two or three years ago, but now appear to drag. Equally, there are plenty of 386SX machines well up to the task of word processing and basic accounting. You must decide how hard you'll work you computer—both now and in the future—and buy accordingly.

In the next chapter we'll take a look at Windows itself. This isn't meant to be a tutorial, it is meant to provide an understanding of the way Windows works.

5

Why Windows works the way it does—and how to exploit it

This chapter is not a Windows tutorial. You'll find a very good tutorial within Windows itself. In Program Manager, choose Help from the drop-down menu, for the Tutorial. The Tutorial will provide you with hands-on experience and a basic understanding of Windows.

This chapter examines the reasons why Windows is designed the way it is. Most introductions to Windows tell you enough to get started; they don't deal with the philosophy behind the program. As a result, you will run the program for a while, until something happens that you don't understand. The purpose of this chapter is to fill in the gaps in your knowledge. In addition, there are useful tips on other aspects of operating Windows.

It's Not DOS with Pretty Pictures

Windows is not DOS with pretty pictures; it's one program that does many things. Windows provides the interface that you see, as well as the icons that you click. Windows programs are written in snippets of code, thus Windows provides the *glue* that connects the code snippets together, and creates many of the things you see on your screen.

Windows manages memory; it makes your RAM available to programs, without using DOS's complicated extended and expanded memory. Windows manages fonts, while it displays them accurately on the screen, and in any size with no loss of detail.

Windows makes it possible for you to connect one or several printers and makes them available to all of your applications, in the same way it makes your fonts available to all of your programs. Windows handles the mouse, and creates virtual memory (part of your hard disk that programs use as RAM when you run out of the real thing).

Windows imposes a universal interface on its programs. You will see the same File and Edit commands in the same place in nearly every program. The program has common keyboard shortcuts such as ALT-F4, which closes programs, and F1, which gets you help. You can cut information from one Windows program and paste it into another.

Windows has a graphics format .BMP that allows you to place graphics in almost any program. It has the ability to insert *objects* from one program into another, so that you can double-click on the object and then open the creating program in order to edit. Windows associates files with the program that created them, or any program on your computer. For example, a WordPerfect file will open in Word for Windows.

Windows has a rudimentary form of multi-tasking that lets you run several programs at once. They can be large or small. I'm running

Word for Windows, as well as Clock and Adobe Type Manager on my computer, and probably parts of other programs of which I'm not even aware.

There are many other strengths of Windows—so many that most people never take full advantage of them. The whole program, even without the *applets* like Write, Paintbrush, and so on, is very complex. Microsoft doesn't help this by making Windows as versatile as possible.

Too much versatility?

Here's an example of Windows' versatility, as compared to the Apple Macintosh. One of the Windows accessories is a clock. The clock can be made visible or not, analog or digital, and take any size or assume any position on the screen. To move or size the clock display, I use either the mouse or the keyboard. Seconds or the date, may be displayed, or I can choose from any of the fonts installed on the computer. I can remove the title from the windows, so that all that is displayed is the time. The clock window can be set to be *always on top*, so that it appears in the same position in every Windows application.

The Macintosh doesn't have a clock.

The intent behind the design of many other Graphical Users Interfaces (GUIs), such as the Macintosh, was to shield the user from much of the complexity of the system. Windows, on the other hand, offers so many options that it appears very complicated, since almost everything you want to do in Windows can be done several different ways. It is possible to run much of Windows without a mouse, though why anyone would want to do that is beyond me.

Due to this overdose of options, you can expect to come across parts of Windows that you don't understand and don't need to understand. Nevertheless, buried in Windows are the commands Microsoft forgot. They put them in the program and then expected you to find and take advantage of them. These *buried* commands are what the remaining chapters of this book are about.

The "Secret" Is that There Are No Secrets

One dangerous assumption is that Windows has some simple setting that just needs to be altered to speed everything up. This assumption isn't dispelled by Windows storing your preferences in Initialization files; the two largest of which are WIN.INI and SYSTEM.INI. Although all GUIs have similar files, Windows has to store these as DOS files, which makes them open to anyone who wants to take a look. A sample of WIN.INI is shown in figure 5-1—gripping stuff, eh?

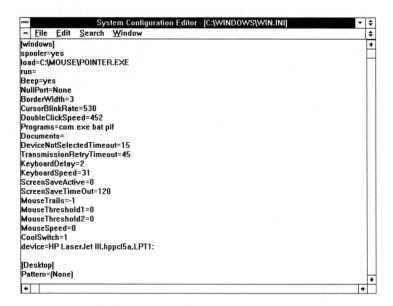

Figure 5-1. The fascinating world of WIN.INI.

Enough people want to know what it all means, and there are now several books that describe every line in your WIN.INI and SYSTEM.INI. Unfortunately, each book has one of three comments after almost every entry, they are as follows:

96

- Don't alter this

- You can alter this to see a small improvement under some rare circumstances

- This setting is more easily altered from the Windows Control Panel

In other words, don't bother.

As Windows is full of information that isn't obvious at first glance, there has been a proliferation of books, magazine articles, and seminars that supposedly explain Windows *secrets*. We all like to know secrets, but when they're as boring as most of the more arcane Windows commands, they're hardly worth knowing.

The magical "SetWindowsSpeed = 0.5" line

However, this hasn't stopped some people from believing that deep in WIN.INI there's a command like SetWindowsSpeed = 0.5, which if you alter to SetWindowsSpeed = 1, will make the program run twice as fast. These seekers after *secrets* don't seem to wonder why Microsoft would include such a command, why they'd keep it a secret, or why it's not yet common knowledge after 30 million copies have been sold.

The fact is that with the default settings, installed in the simplest way, Windows achieves at least 95 per cent of the speed that most users can ever get from it. In rare circumstances that don't relate to everyday activities, some of these settings can be changed to get better performance. Yet, people who don't know what they're doing can change settings so that Windows runs slower.

Actually, the real way to speed up Windows is to accelerate the way you interact with the program, and to do the things you must to discover what happens when Windows runs.

97

What's happening in Windows

When you run Windows, Program Manager is always operating. In addition to Program Manager, other programs run simultaneously. As a result, whenever you see anything other than Program Manager, you will have other software running in windows of their own. At the moment, the window on my screen is showing Word for Windows, which covers the Program Manager window. Microsoft states that Word for Windows is on top of Program Manager, although some DTP and graphics programs use the term *in front of*.

Even Program Manager is *on top* of the Windows desktop, which is the screen you see when Windows starts up; if you have wallpaper, this is where it will be seen. If Program Manager doesn't cover the entire screen, you can still see part of the desktop in the background. If you run Program Manager at full screen all the time, you may not realize that there's anything behind it.

This isn't a problem unless you accidentally minimize a program (by clicking in the gray square with the downward pointing triangle found in the top right-hand part of the screen). The now minimized icon is on the desktop, behind Program Manager, and to a novice it looks like the application just vanished. To retrieve it, you must go back to Program Manager, minimize it if necessary, and then double-click on the application's icon.

Sizing windows

When you run an application, it normally has an *application window*, and a *document window* within. You can tell if this is the case by looking at the top right-hand corner of your screen. If there are two gray squares, one above the other, and each has a triangle pointing upward above another pointing downward, you have a document window inside an application window. Additionally, both are displayed in maximum size. These squares are called buttons and are shown in figure 5-2.

98

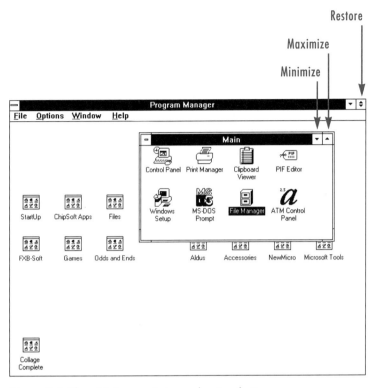

Figure 5-2. The minimize, maximize, and restore buttons.

Maximized application windows fill the screen; maximized document windows fill the application window, whatever size the window has taken. Application windows may be changed to one of the following three sizes:

- Minimized, where all you see is an normal-size icon

- An intermediate size, being the last size at which you left it

- Maximized, where the application covers the screen

Document windows can only be intermediate or maximized, except in File Manager. Whenever a document window is intermediate size, you will notice that the menu bar remains as part of the application window.

99

Normally you will view an application in one of five views:

- Minimized, this contains the icon, the name of the program, and the name of the file

- Intermediate application, intermediate document

- Intermediate application, maximized document

- Maximized application, intermediate document

- Maximized application, maximized document

Once a document is maximized, it expands to fill the extra space when you maximize an application window.

The buttons tell you what you can do with a window.

- Minimize button—convert this application to an icon

- Restore button—convert an application or document window to its intermediate size

- Maximize button—increase an application window to fill the screen, or increase a document window to fill the application window

Get Some Hands On

If you want to see how all this works, try these exercises.

1. Open an application. Most Windows applications let you open documents in windows, but Write and Paintbrush—two of the applets that come with windows—do not. You need to open an application with a document window, which has two buttons, one above the other, in the top right-hand corner of the screen.

2. Click on both buttons so that the application and the document are running at full screen. This may already be the

case—if so, both buttons display two triangles each, like the Word for Windows example in figure 5-3 following.

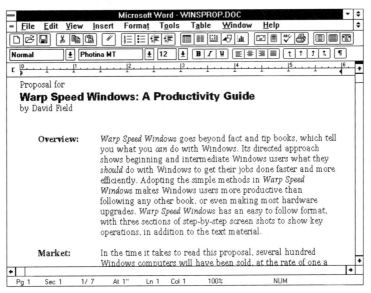

Figure 5-3. Word for Windows is maximized, and so is the document.

3. Now, click on the top button that points down to reduce the size of the application window. It will become smaller, but the document still fills the inside of the window.

4. Now, click the lower button (pointing down) to reduce the size of the document window. The window becomes smaller. Drag on one edge of the document window to reduce its size even further.

5. Notice both widows now have a maximize button (with one upward-pointing triangle), and the application window also has a minimize button, (one downward-pointing triangle). Your screen should resemble figure 5-4 following.

101

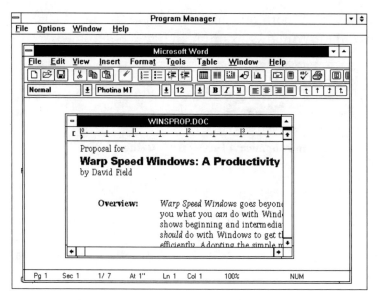

Figure 5-4. The same program and file as figure 5-3, but both application and document windows are at intermediate size.

6. Click on the **maximize** button for the document window. It fills the application window. Now click on the document window's **restore** button, and it reduces to the size you gave it in step 4.

7. Click on the **maximize** button for the application window. The application window opens to full-screen, but the document window remains the same size.

8. Double-click in the **title bar** of the application (where you can read the name of the application). This reduces the window to its intermediate size. Now double-click again, and the window fills the screen.

9. Double-click in the **document window title bar** to expand it to fill the application window.

As these exercises demonstrate, double-clicking in the title bar of a window is the same as clicking on the maximize or restore buttons, and it's an easier target.

Some applications allow you more than one document open at once. Consequently, you may get one application window with several document windows inside. In order to select the document you want to work on, click anywhere inside its window. This *active window* has a colored border and title bar.

You may also click on **File** in the Menu bar and hit one of the buttons located at the top left-hand corner of the screen. Unless you don't have a mouse, you can safely ignore these buttons and their menus. One or two applications have special commands, but generally these menus simply resize the window through menu commands, and duplicate the functions of the buttons located at the top right-hand corner of the screen.

Where did my program go?

Now we'll *lose* an application.

1. If Program Manager is not already maximized, maximize it.

2. Open **Write** from the Accessories group.

3. Type a few characters and then go to the File menu.

4. Select **Save As.** In the resulting dialog box, name the file **Test.**

5. Click on the **Minimize** button. Write disappears—is it lost?

6. Program Manager appears. Open **Paintbrush** from the Accessories group.

7. If Paintbrush doesn't already fill the screen, **Maximize** it.

103

8. Click on the **Restore** button in Paintbrush. Paintbrush only fills part of the screen.

9. If you can see it, click on the restore button in Program Manager. If Paintbrush covers the button, click in the **title bar** of Paintbrush and drag it away.

10. The windows desktop appears, with a Write icon with Write—Test beneath it. You may have to drag Paintbrush or Program Manager up the screen to see this icon. You can see an example in figure 5-5.

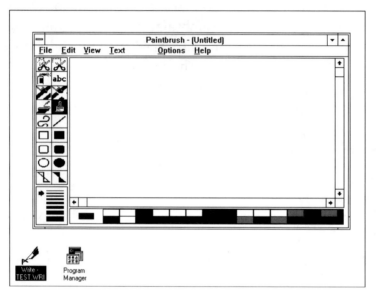

Figure 5-5. Where your "lost" program went to.

11. Double-click on the **Write** icon to restore your Write document to the stage it was before step 5.

As you've just demonstrated, minimized applications appear to be lost, but are just waiting on the desktop for a double-click behind Program Manager. If you wanted to, you could minimize Write once again and Paintbrush as well. Both icons will appear on the desktop, and display at full-screen with a double-click.

Programs as icons

What happened to Write when it was an icon? The answer is: nothing. The only change that occurred was the way in which it was displayed. Full-screen, intermediate, or minimized—it's crucial that you understand that a program whether it is full-screen, intermediate, or minimized still carries on as before. Since programs don't run for long without some user action, most programs reduced to icons are in suspended animation. You must make them occupy all or part of the screen before you can do something new.

If a program is doing some long task that requires no input from you, it can carry on quite happily as an icon. You can minimize your communications program while it downloads a file from a bulletin board, or bring another window to the front of your screen while the computer is doing something else. Since the CPU is trying to do two things at once, you may not be able to run the new program as fast as you'd like, but it will still run in the foreground while the other program runs in the background.

What's also useful is the ability to have a program open and running whenever you need it. Suppose you decide to resume work on a word processing file you last dealt with some weeks ago. You go to open it, but it doesn't appear to be in the list of files in the Open dialog box. You could waste time by quitting the application and opening File Manager to look for it, or you could switch directly to File Manager, locate the missing file, and immediately return to your word processor.

This time-wasting method is the way you'd have to do things in DOS, which lets you run only one program at a time (apart from a few TSR programs). Windows is set up to multi-task. With four megabytes of RAM and virtual memory you can run just about anything you need. You'll learn how to do this later in the book.

Menus and Dialog Boxes

For a user, the main difference between Windows and DOS is the drop-down menus. Because very few programs have keyboard shortcuts for every command, most users drop down a menu and select a command. While this is certainly advisable when you are new to an application, as you become more accustomed the commands you should start to use keyboard shortcuts.

Using the keyboard for some commands speeds up your work. It takes time to move your hand across to the mouse, move the cursor to the menu item, and then select the command from the list. Don't feel you have to use keyboard shortcuts for more commands than those with which you're comfortable. It's easier to make a mistake by selecting key combinations than when you see the command. If you're unsure, use the menu.

Some commands in dialog boxes appear in gray rather than dark type. This means that they are not available at a particular moment. If you open an application, but do no work in it, there is nothing to save. Consequently, the Save command is gray. Any command followed by ellipses (...) means that it opens a dialog box. Some commands have a triangle pointing to the right, indicating a submenu of commands. A checkmark to the left of the command means something has been selected—usually an on-screen aid such as toolbar.

You will have to make your own choices about toolbars, ribbons, rulers, and other on-screen items. While they make it easy to apply changes to your work, they may also obscure it. I prefer to have as many of these on-screen helps available as possible, but you may find they get in the way. If you are familiar with the program and use only a few commands, you can get by without them. Remember certain applications may have originated on the Macintosh, and these will have been created to work on the Mac Classic's nine inch screen where space is at a premium. In contrast, your monitor is likely to be at least 14 inches diagonally.

Finding Out More About Your Programs

There are many wonderful features in programs; you just need to look at the menus to see the many possibilities. One problem is that commands like Repaginate Now can be cryptic. Are the commands you try to use useful, or do they cause you to lose work? If you don't know what a command does, don't use it! The average person uses only 30 percent of the commands in a program.

You can learn more about a program without losing work, although it's best to investigate when you don't have a vital file open. All dialog boxes have a Cancel button, so you can try a command without changing a file. The settings in a dialog box often give you an idea of what task the dialog box performs.

Many Windows programs have context-sensitive help. If you select a command you're not familiar with, press **F1** while you still have the command selected, then let go of the mouse button. You will probably see a help box with information on the command. Unfortunately, not every application has this kind of help, and you may find that all you receive is the general help window. Some applications let you press **Shift-F1,** which turns the cursor into a question mark. If you click on anything, the relevant help information appears on the screen.

Many applications also have their own tutorial. Look under the help menu and you may see a command for Tutorial or Getting Started. Don't bother with *About* ...; it's just a simple dialog box telling you the version of the program and other details. If you didn't install the program yourself the person who did may not have taken the time to install the tutorial files; thus, you may have to go through the install routine in order to be able to use them.

Windows Control Panel

The Windows Control Panel lets you set many of the features that affect the way you work. Although there's a bewildering number of choices, you will probably only need to set a few.

Colors. This is shown in figure 5-6. Although some displays look like someone put something funny in the Kool-Aid, I prefer **Pastel**. If you play with custom color schemes, you can end up with white text on a white background—not exactly conducive to easy reading. There are also color schemes designed specifically for portable computers. The standard Windows default scheme has always struck me as a little cold.

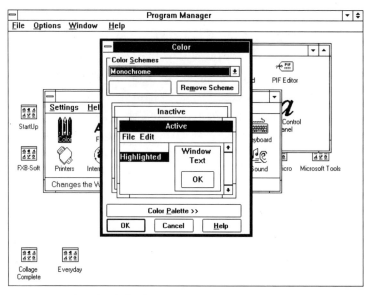

Figure 5-6. The color dialog box.

Mouse. This comes in two flavors—the basic Windows dialog box, and the more complex dialog box that comes with the Microsoft mouse, shown in figure 5-7 (to follow). If you have either set of mouse controls, you can make some changes to the way in which you use the mouse. The most important is the double-clicking

108

speed. If you're new to using a mouse you may have trouble double-clicking. This is usually because you move the mouse between clicks, and may not be clicking fast enough. Try double-clicking in the area marked *TEST*. If you have trouble, move the slider button a little to the left and try again.

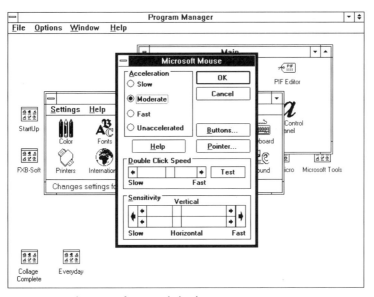

Figure 5-7. The Microsoft mouse dialog box.

You may have problems when you run out of space and off the edge of the mouse pad. You probably realize that you can lift the mouse back into the center of the pad without moving the cursor. What you may not know, however, is that the mouse has acceleration—that is, the faster you move the mouse over an inch of mouse pad, the greater distance the cursor travels on the screen. Experienced users are accustomed to this and place the mouse without a second thought. Beginners tend to nervously move the mouse slowly across the pad and run out of space. The key is to move the mouse quickly to the general area where you want it, then move slowly to the exact spot. Incidentally, the selected point is located at the the very tip of the pointer or the top left of the cursor.

There's another setting in the mouse dialog box—mouse trails (or as some call it, *mouse droppings*). If you have a portable computer the cursor is hard to see; selecting the mouse trails option makes the cursor leave a visible trail of pointers. With a genuine Microsoft mouse, the dialog box gives you more options, and one that suits me is the larger cursor. Try it for yourself.

Date & Time. This feature, shown in figure 5-8, is fairly obvious; it lets you set the date and time. Computer clocks are rarely accurate, so you should check the clock every couple of weeks. Some, by accident or laziness, have a system clock that's days off; it's not a problem until you look for the file saved last Tuesday morning, which is stored with a date of the previous Thursday afternoon.

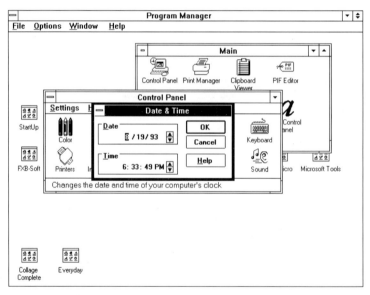

Figure 5-8. The dialog box to set date and time.

Printers. A typical example of the dialog box is found in figure 5-9. This is where you tell Windows which printer you have by telling it which printer drivers to use. In theory, most non-networked users have one printer. In practice, it's not as simple at this. With one printer, I manage to have five printer drivers from which to choose.

One of these is a mistake; some program installed the driver for the HPGL plotter. There's the driver for the actual printer, which is a Hewlett-Packard LaserJet III. In addition, I added a LaserMaster WinPrinter card. Consequently, there are drivers for the 300 dots-per-inch direct mode, and another for the 800 dots-per- inch PostScript mode. Finally, the Micrografx Graphics Works program has installed the Micrografx PostScript driver, a much better alternative to the Windows PostScript drivers. It would be preferable if I had a printer with its own PostScript capability.

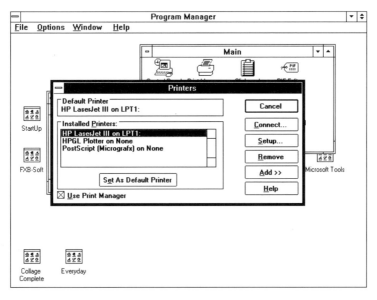

Figure 5-9. Setting a printer.

Desktop. The Desktop feature is the place to make alterations to your desktop; some are obvious, some less so. Take a look at figure 5-10. I don't have wallpaper or a screen saver; wallpaper is something you see once in a while, if at all, and while it may be fun to play with, ultimately it gets boring. I've tried to do too many things on other people's machines to ever want to see a screen saver again. I'm tired of watching the screen as a long process executes, only to have flying toasters interrupt at the critical point.

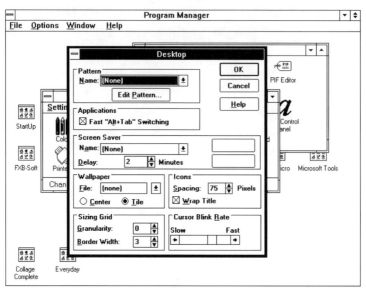

Figure 5-10. Changing the desktop.

There are two boxes that you must check; usually these are checked as part of the Windows default setup. Under Applications, check **Fast Alt+Tab** switching, and under Icons, check **Wrap Title.** These two settings form the basis of the methods shown in subsequent chapters of this book, which I will discuss in greater detail later.

Fonts. You may add TrueType format fonts here (see figure 5-11). If you have Adobe format (Type 1) fonts, you will need Adobe Type Manager, which is in the Main group in Program Manager (see figure 5-12). There are some questionable choices offered in the the TrueType dialog boxes; ignore these options, and always keep the **Copy to Windows** directory box checked. Why anyone would choose either to not display TrueType fonts, display only TrueType fonts, or have the font files on their hard drive without installing them is beyond me.

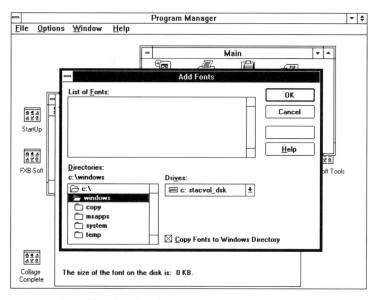

Figure 5-11. Adding TrueType fonts.

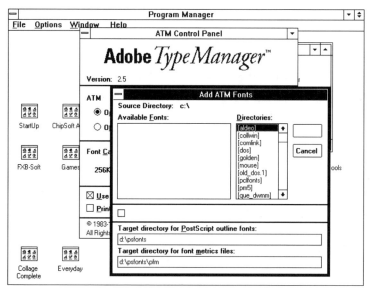

Figure 5-12. The Adobe Type manager dialog box.

113

Once you have installed fonts in either format, they are in theory available to all Windows applications. Some programs, like PageMaker's Table Editor, can't handle a large selection of font choices and choose a few, seemingly at random. If your program can handle both formats you can mix and match them if you choose, letter by letter.

Working Faster in File Manager

Some points about File Manager haven't had the exposure they deserve. One task you will carry out fairly regularly is moving and copying files. If you drag file icons within the disk (or disk partition) Windows assumes you want to move them. If you drag the icons from one disk to another Windows assumes you want to copy them.

To copy efficiently, for example from drive C to a diskette in drive B, you can move the file icons up to the drive icon at the top of the File Manager window. Since, you rarely make directories on floppy disks, the files end up where you would expect—on B. If you try to do the same thing but want to copy files from Drive B to Drive C, the files end up in the current directory on C, which may not be the directory you want. In fact, you can copy files from a diskette to a hard drive and then have no idea where they are.

Some people select a drive by clicking once on the drive icon. Don't do this! Each time you do, you're creating another full-screen window for that drive, which will eventually be hidden behind more recent windows. Instead, double-click on the **drive icon.** This opens a drive window that only occupies part of the screen. If the current directory isn't the one you want, you can scroll around the directory window until you find the correct directory. Now, you'll be certain that the files will end up where you want them.

Another problem people have is copying certain types of files from a directory. You may want only .DOC files from your Word for Windows directory, for example, but there are about a dozen different file formats. For example, you could choose **Sort by Type** from the View menu; however, you still see all the files in the directory and probably have to scroll to find the group of files you want. A better way is to choose **Select by File Type;** so long as the document box is checked off, you can put *.DOC in the Name field. Now when you look at the directory window, all you will see will be .DOC files. To copy all these files to another disk, choose **Shift-/** (Shift-Slash) to select every file that's visible and then drag one file icon to the new location. All the other files you selected will come with it.

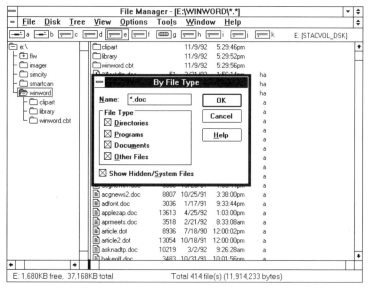

Figure 5-13. File Manager's Select by File Type dialog box.

Copying from diskettes

This approach makes life even easier when copying from multiple diskettes to a hard drive. Here's how to copy.

1. Open the window for the diskette drive.

2. Select **By File Type** and choose the name details to pick up only the files you want (see figure 5-13).

3. Double-click on the hard drive icon, select the target directory, and move this window so you can see the list of files on the diskette.

4. Now insert the first diskette. Make sure that the diskette window is active.

5. Press **Shift-/**. Drag any icon to the target directory. This copies all the files.

6. Remove the diskette and insert the next in the series. Select the diskette window again to make it active, and press the **F5** key. This forces Windows to re-read the drive, so you see the contents of the new diskette.

7. Repeat steps 5 and 6 until you are done.

You can select files by more than just the file extension. If you have a customer called Modern Plumbing Supplies for instance, you can name your files MPSLET01.DOC, MPSBUD01.XLS, and MPSAD001.PM5, so that all projects you do will start with the same three letters. Then just select MPS*.* to copy only files created for this customer, or MPS*.PM5 for just the Pagemaker files.

So far all we've looked at are tips to make some jobs easier. In the next few chapters, we'll be looking at how to configure Windows so that almost every job you do goes faster.

6

Keeping Your Desktop Organized

In this chapter, you'll see how to set up Program Manager so that you can start any program with a mouse click. This may sound obvious, but most setups don't allow this.

Look at the desktop in figure 6-1. It's a typical Windows setup; yours is probably similar. Why is the window so small? When Windows was installed on this machine, Program Manager opened at part screen size, and no one knows how to get it to a full screen. In the meantime, half the screen isn't being used for anything.

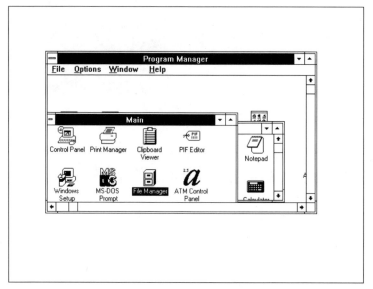

Figure 6-1. A messy desktop.

In fact, if you asked the user how he or she uses the computer, you'd probably get an answer like this:

> "I mainly use it for writing letters and memos, and often I create a report. Now and then I'll make a presentation, and at the end of the month I use my spreadsheet to do expenses–and of course I use it heavily at budget time. Sometimes I send a diskette to the head office. I keep an address list, and once in a while I play Solitaire."

So how does Program Manager carry out these tasks? As it's set up, hardly at all. The open window obscures much of what's left. *Lotus Applications*–is this *Ami Pro, 1-2-3,* or both? What are the other icons for? Surely *Read Me* files are less important than icons that start an application?

Why your Desktop is in a Mess

How did Program Manager get this way? You probably already know. As you install an application, it creates a group in Program Manager. Some applications insist on having their own group. Others will set up a group for applications from the same company. A few will install themselves into existing groups.

Even if you don't have many applications installed on your computer, Windows sets up groups such as Main, Accessories, and StartUp. You may wonder what purpose these groups serve. For instance, why is StartUp empty?

Most people presume there's a reason for this, and accept whatever Program Manager provides. A few, however, decide to bring some order to the chaos. If your Program Manager looks like figure 6-1, here's how to make it look like figure 6-2.

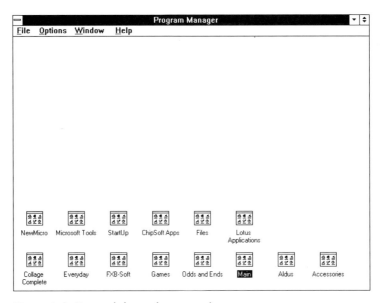

Figure 6-2. Neat and clean—but not much use.

Cleaning Up the Mess

The first thing to do is to press the upward-pointing triangle in the top right-hand corner of the Program manager window. This is the maximize button, and it makes Program Manager fill the screen.

After this, close the open window by pressing the downward-pointing triangle in the top right-hand corner, to the left of the maximize button. This is the minimize button, and the window becomes an icon at the bottom of the screen.

Finally, go to the Window menu and select **Arrange Icons**. This causes the Group icons to move to the bottom of the screen, and arrange themselves in a neat line.

What have we achieved with this?

- All the program group icons are visible

- The full screen is being used

- Adding a new program group won't hide anything else

To use this setup, you double-click on the program group icon, then select the program icon and double-click on that. This takes you into the program. Whenever you exit a program you make sure to close the program group window first.

Improving the setup

There are ways to improve this setup. If you open the program group windows one at a time, you can drag the window (by clicking and dragging in the title bar) and resize it so that it doesn't hide any of the program group icons . This means you don't have to close each window; you can just open one on top of the other. If you want to run a program again, the window is already open, only you'll have to click on a visible part of that window to bring it into view.

120

When a window is in the intermediate stage, neither minimized or maximized, Windows remembers the size and location of the window from session to session. When you select the intermediate size, it will be in the same place as last time; you can vary this by dragging the window or a border or corner to change it. This will become the new intermediate window. You'll probably notice that Windows automatically installs scroll bars if the window can't show all its icons.

What You See When You Start Up

What determines what you see when you start up Windows? There are two ways to affect this; one is fairly useless, so is easily available from a menu. The other is effective, but needs a special command and is almost undocumented.

You can select **Save Settings on Exit** from the Options menu; if there's a check mark to the left of the name, it's selected. Each time you quit Windows, whatever the state of your Program Manager screen, it will come back in exactly the same form. If you dutifully close program groups at the end of every session, you'll be rewarded with a neat screen on startup. Of course, if you forget, you'll get the same messy screen you closed on the last time you used Windows.

The sensible way to keep your screen the way you want it is to close all program groups, then hold down the **Shift** key and select **Exit Windows** from the File menu. You don't actually exit Windows, but exactly the same screen greets you every time you start up the program–unless you have **Save Settings on Exit** selected. So what seemed to be the solution turns out to be a problem. Any time you want to alter your settings, just change them and choose **Shift-Exit Windows** again.

It is unclear why Microsoft chose this way of recording your screen setup. The Shift-Exit Windows command isn't on the File menu, nor can I find it in Program Manager Help. It does feature it in the manual, but most beginners would be worried about selecting Exit anything, for fear that they really would leave Windows.

Keeping it neat

There are two more commands on the Options menu; Auto Arrange and Minimize on Use. The former is useful, the latter is not. Auto Arrange is worth keeping on all the time; as it makes all your icons in Group windows arrange themselves neatly in the top left-hand corner of the window. This command is similar Arrange Icons on the Windows menu, except that it works automatically. The only time you'll need Arrange Icons is when you want to put your Group Icons into line.

If you're not using Auto Arrange, turn it on now. Since your icons take up the minimum of space, you can resize open windows to make them as small as possible. There's less chance of them over-lapping each other, or your losing one of them in a far-off corner of the window. You may also arrange your icons so that they don't leave unused space in the window. For example, if you have nine icons, you waste space if they're arranged in a line of six over a line of three. Move the bottom window border down to accommodate an extra line of icons, then move the right-hand border in until the window is three icons wide. The icons will Auto Arrange them-selves in the window.

What does Minimize on Use do, and why don't you need it? This set-ting reduces Program Manager to an icon whenever you start an appli-cation. If your application opens in part-screen view, you may see the Program Manager icon at any time. If you double-click on the icon, it will reopen Program Manager and let you choose other applications.

Why is this a problem? First, when you exit the application Program Manager remains an icon–you have to double-click on it in order to open it up and do anything useful. You must lose space from your application window to display the Program Manager icon. Some applications automatically open at full-screen, so you'll have to reduce these to the intermediate size to get any benefit from this arrangement. Finally, Alt-Tab provides a much more efficient way of getting to Program Manager when you're in an application. I'll cover this in a later chapter.

Our mythical user is doing better. All those applications are a couple of mouse clicks away; nothing obscures anything else, all appears to be functioning properly. Nevertheless this isn't the end of the search. Why should we need to open program groups every time?

The next step

The customary method by which most people get around this is to open some of the more important windows and move them around so they don't overlap. Then applications are just a mouse-click away. For the first time, another person can see exactly what applications are installed on the computer—at least, those in the opened windows. This is a simple version of the two ways in which Windows manages opened windows.

Cascading windows

You can position opened windows automatically. To do this, you'll find commands on the Window menu–**Cascade** and **Tile.** Cascade is probably the less successful. Since it takes all open windows and makes them the same size, each almost overlapping the previous one. You can see the title bars and a thin section of the left-hand side of the window. The windows appear to cascade down from the top left of your screen.

Only one window is fully visible; to view what's in the others you need to click on any part (other than the buttons) and that window moves to the front. This means that some windows then have their title bars obscured. If you have more than seven windows (on a 14 inch monitor) the extras completely cover some of the other windows–so completely that you probably wouldn't be aware that there were any other windows behind them. The cascade eventually covers any unopened group icons along the bottom of your screen.

The main reason for this is that the windows are so large. Each can hold around 18 icons–way too many for the average application window. If all you can see of a window is its title bar, you should work with a row of unopened windows along the bottom of Program Manager. If you want to see how Cascade appears on your computer, be warned; the size and position of the windows now become the default. If you minimize the windows they'll open up later in the same size and position as they did in Cascade; you'll have to move and resize them if you don't want them to overlap.

Tiling windows

Tiling seems to be the answer to this problem. This takes your open windows and makes them as large as possible without overlapping–just like laying down a set of tiles. When you select **Tile** from the Window menu the program even checks to see if you have any unopened Group icons, and leaves the bottom part of the screen uncovered if this is the case.

Now that you've opened every window you want, if the windows can't display all their icons they will display a scroll bar. Most of your application icons are visible; if not, you may quickly scroll to see them. Anyone who has to use your machine can see which applications you've installed. You can control the position of windows, either by dragging them around the screen, or by minimizing everything and then opening them up in order; the last window opened will be in the top left, the first opened at bottom right.

Improving Tiling

However, not everything in the garden is rosy. Some windows have plenty of empty space; others need scroll bars. If you have a large number of windows, the amount of space for each usually isn't large enough. If a new application creates a new group window, you have to retile your screen. You will still have to choose the icon that actually launches the program.

You may control how much space each window receives by resizing it, and you can reduce windows with one or two icons and use the space to increase the size of more populated windows. For instance, if you have five open windows, Program Manager makes two larger windows and three smaller ones; you can use the method described above to open windows in order so that the most populated windows are allotted the most space. If you want to see what Tiling looks like, the same warning applies as in Cascade; the tiled windows are now the new intermediate size.

The Secret of Setting Up Program Manager

Every one of these methods assumes an incorrect approach, they each focus on the wrong thing–the program group. What's important is the applications icon. That's the reason why Tiling doesn't work very well; populated windows don't have many application-launching icons, they are full of Read Me and installer files. The crux of setting up Program Manager efficiently is displaying only the icons that launch programs.

Retrieving icons

At this point some people worry about manipulating icons around Program Manager. There's one hard and fast rule about Program Manager–you cannot delete programs or files while you're in it. You can delete the icons representing them, but there's no change to your hard disk (apart from the stored information about Program Manager's configuration, of course).

If you accidentally delete the icon that starts your favorite application, go to Windows Setup in the Main window. Under the Options menu choose **SetUp Applications,** and you'll see the dialog box shown in figure 6-3. If you don't know the name of the file, you may choose **Search for applications** and add the application to the list. You may also select **Specify an application.** You'll be asked to name the application you want to set up and be asked to enter the DOS path. If you don't know the path, click the **Browse** button to look for the file.

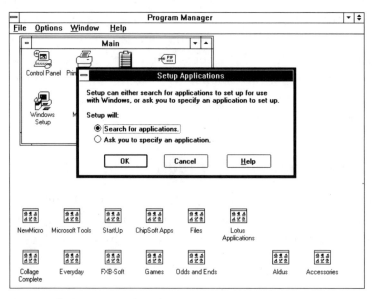

Figure 6-3. Setting up applications.

Another way of retrieving an application icon is to open File Manager and reduce it to intermediate size, so that an open Group window is partly visible behind it. Now drag the application file (which usually ends in .EXE) from File Manager into the Group window. There it magically gains a full-size icon (see figure 6-4). You'll see how to get the correct application name (Word for Windows instead of WINWORD.EXE).

126

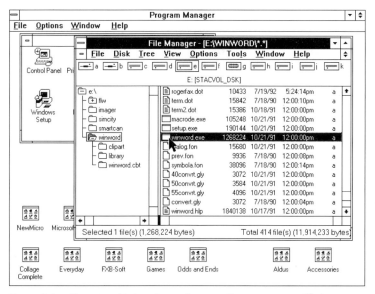

Figure 6-4. Dragging this icon into a Program Manager group will give you a Word for Windows icon.

To rearrange Program Manager, you must accept that there's nothing sacred about the Program groups in Windows. You can add new groups, delete old groups, combine groups or split them apart. It also makes sense to set up Program Manager so that you work most efficiently; but it shouldn't be so strange that someone who has to work on your computer can't understand how it's organized.

Creating your most important group

Let's look again at that mythical user we met at the beginning of this chapter. Who uses a word processor, presentation graphics, a spreadsheet, and a personal information manager–along with Solitaire. Let's make using them easier. Create a new Program Group, by choosing **New** on the File Menu and selecting Program Group. Name this **Everyday.**

Only move the icons that start your favorite programs into this window. All you need to do is open the windows where they're cur-

127

rently found and drag them across to the new window. Our mythical user would do this with the four business application icons, along with Solitaire. Now close all other windows, move this new window to the center of your screen, and size it so that every icon is visible. Finally, hold down the **Shift** key and select **Exit Windows** to make this the default screen.

From now on, every time you open Windows you'll see only the icons you need. One double-click and you're into the program. You'll never have to search for missing icons or close windows to see what's underneath them.

If you install a new application you can drag the new icon out of the Group window and into your Applications window. Then close the Group window and **Shift-Exit Windows** to make a new default screen.

Accommodating other people

If other people use your machine, you may find it necessary to add other icons so that every major application on your computer is represented . If someone says "You can use Carmen's computer, she's on vacation," it doesn't help if the application they want is buried in a Group window somewhere, because Carmen never uses it. Add the icons for these applications to your Applications window; just keep your special applications in the top row.

It may be that your organization has a standard range of applications which must appear on every computer. In this case you can copy icons instead of dragging them. Just **Control-drag** and the original icon remains in place. If people use your computer expecting to find the same groups in the same places, you'd be better off copying the icons rather than moving them. Double-clicking on a copied icon is the same as working with the original–in fact, it's impossible to tell which is which.

Although I describe a better way of using File Manager later in the book, it's a good idea to copy the icon if you intend to put it in your

Applications window. Many believe that File Manager is found only in the Main window, so even if it's staring them in the face they'll look for it in Main. Make a copy of it. The same is true if you're using something from the Accessories group.

You may have noticed that I stress keeping the computer intelligible to other users In an organization, where several people may use the same computer at one time or another, this is a given. But even if it's your own home computer, it's a good idea to keep icons in predictable places. You may want to sell the computer to someone who's a little unsure of Windows; if your Windows screen looks odd, you may lose the sale. You might need to take the machine to the repair shop; will they waste time working out how to test it? Of course you never know if you'll be away from home and have to get someone else to take an important file from the computer.

The next most important program group

If you like this idea of one Program group to hold your applications, why not take the idea a step further and have only one other window to hold all the icons that have been added to Program Manager? This seems as straightforward as making the Applications window, but there are a few traps.

Icon titles may seem fully descriptive when they're in a window with an application name, but lose their identity if they're mixed with other similar files. An obvious example is Read Me. Most applications come with an icon with this name. If this is in the Excel Window, it refers to Excel, but will you remember what it means when it's in a generic window, with half-a-dozen other files called Read Me?

Worse are icons called Installer or Setup. These usually come with an icon showing a diskette drive and a diskette, no matter what program they work with. For many programs if you need to add certain new features, you must use their installer program. It may take quite a bit of time working out which installer goes with which program.

The solution is to rename the icons. They will still start the same programs as before, but you may call them Ami Pro Read Me, PageMaker 5 Installer, and so forth. You may also notice these titles don't bear much resemblance to DOS filename conventions. This is because they use one of the under-utilized features of Windows, the Description Property.

Using Properties

If you open a window and highlight an icon, you may see more details of the icon in Properties, on the File menu. Select the File Manager (but do not open it!). When you choose Properties, you'll see the Program Item Properties dialog box similar to figure 6-5.

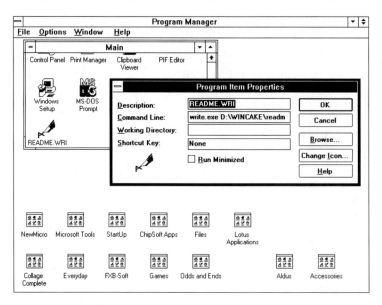

Figure 6-5. This file is an anonymous README, but the Properties dialog box shows it's from the WINCAKE directory for the Cakewalk application.

The first two windows are the most important. Under **Description** you can type a new description, which can be up to forty characters with spaces. So instead of having that file just be another anonymous Read Me, it can be Excel Read Me. The directory WINCAKE was set up by the music program Cakewalk, so I renamed the icon Cakewalk Readme (see figure 6-6). Just type the new description in the **Description** box and it appears in Program Manager, as in figure 6-7.

The Program Item Properties dialog box gives you almost complete power over any icon you display. You may be so used to clicking on the same old icons to bring up the same old programs that you've forgotten that Windows is actually a shell–a highly efficient shell— but still a vehicle for automating DOS.

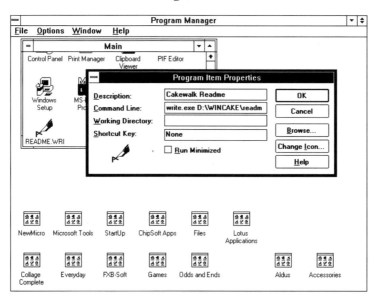

Figure 6-6. Entering a new name for the icon.

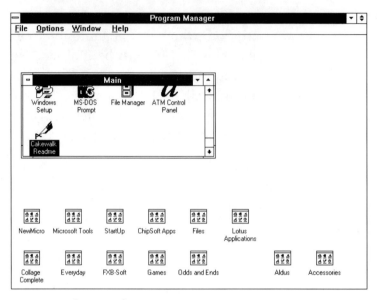

Figure 6-7. The icon with a new name.

The Program Item Properties dialog box controls what the icon stands for. You can:

- Change the description under the icon;

- Change the command line which tells DOS which program to launch;

- Change the working directory (the directory where you open and save);

- Change the icon;

- Make a shortcut key combination to launch the program, and

- Make the program start up but run as an icon until you need it.

132

Now your files can have forty-character names

If you're used to DOS' clunky *eight characters, no spaces* way of naming files, you'll be in seventh heaven with the Description line. You may enter up to forty characters; put spaces between words, and use all those forbidden characters DOS won't allow. You may even use the extended character set by holding down ALT and typing a four-digit number (for example ALT- 0189 gives a true 1/2 character).

In the next chapter you'll see how to alter the command line so that you can open applications and files as well, all with one mouse click. For now, be aware that you can put in any command DOS will accept. Not many pure DOS commands will work here. There's nothing to stop you from entering the command line for a different program, so that your Excel icons gives the command C:\WIN-WORD\WINWORD.EXE (which starts up Word for Windows). This is hardly useful, but it shows you that a command line isn't tied to a particular icon.

If you keep your files in another directory from the executable files (the files that actually run the program), the Working Directory section lets you enter it here. As soon as you go to Open or Save, this is the directory you'll see. The shortcut key combination must work with all the other programs you run, otherwise you'll go to start a program and invoke a macro by mistake. In Chapter Five you'll see how to use the advantages of the **Run Minimized** button. If you have this checked when you click on the icon the application is open, but only as an icon, and won't display in front of the program on which you're working on.

Finally, the **Change Icon** button does exactly that. There are many icons of which you're probably not aware, scattered throughout your files. Many applications have alternate icons, and there are large numbers of spare icons in two files in your Windows directory— PROGMAN.EXE and MORICONS.DLL. Click the **Change Icon** but-

133

ton. You may see more than one icon in the resulting dialog box. Click on your choice to change the icon.

If you don't see more than one icon, select **Browse** and choose one of the two icon files I mentioned above. When you've picked your icon click on it and choose **OK** to return to the Program Item Properties dialog box. You can always repeat the process if you decide you don't like the icon.

One handy use for the Program Item Properties dialog box is to make a new item. Control-drag any icon to make a copy. Enter a new **Description, Command Line,** and **Working Directory** (make this the same as the command line directory if you don't store your files in special directories). Now choose an icon, and you have a functional icon for Program Manager.

Getting an Icon Back

If you accidentally delete an icon you can rebuild it. Suppose that by mistake you've deleted the icon for Word for Windows. Here's how to get it back:

1. **Control-drag** any icon to copy.

2. Choose **Properties** and open the dialog box.

3. Enter **Microsoft Word** in the **Description** section.

4. Place an insertion point in the **Command Line** section, and press **Browse.**

5. Navigate to the Winword directory. Select **WINWORD.EXE.** and choose **OK.**

6. Type in the Working Directory. It will be the same directory that holds WINWORD.EXE, unless you choose to keep your files elsewhere.

7. Click on **Change Icon,** Select the **Word for Windows** Icon, choose **OK.**

8. Choose **OK** from the Program Items Properties dialog box, and you'll have a working **Word for Windows** icon.

You can use the Properties dialog box to change things about icon descriptions that you don't like. Microsoft calls the icon for Word for Windows *Microsoft Word.* You may access the Properties box and change the name if you prefer. I regularly delete the exclamation points and capital letters in the Corel applications, so that I have icons staidly labeled *Corel Draw,* not *Corel DRAW!*

In this chapter you've begun to tap the hidden powers of Windows to create a screen which shows all your applications on startup in order. A program is never more than a mouse-click away. But this isn't all Windows can do–it's just the beginning. In the next chapter, you'll see how the Program Items Properties dialog box lets you create file icons, so that you can open a document and the program that created it with a single mouse-click.

7

Advanced Desktop, with File Icons and a Handy Clock

In this chapter you'll learn how to set up icons which start a program running, You'll also be shown how to open a file without using the Open dialog box, and view the date at any time in any application.

One of the more important functions of an operating system is to provide access to your files. You may need to return to a file for several reasons; you couldn't finish all the work in one session, you need to use a file as the basis for a new job, or you must refer to something done some time ago.

Windows accomplishes this either through File Manager, or by browsing the list in your application's Open dialog box. There's a better way to get at your files, but before I show you this, we need to look at the whole business of how you work with files.

The Different Kinds of Data Files

You work on files for numerous reasons. The three reasons outlined above describe *current work*, since you're still trying to create something when you use the file.

However, you also work with files for storage. You may want to move a file to another directory, put it on a floppy disk to give to someone else, or delete it because you don't need it any more. These uses may be described as housekeeping, since you don't actually achieve anything by working with the files, other than keeping your computer house in order.

Finally, you can move files onto a storage medium and keep them somewhere removed from the computer. You may do this to guard against hard disk failure; this is called backup. You may just want to clear files off the disk to make space; this is called archiving.

Now that hard drives can be hundreds of megabytes in size, there is a great temptation to use your hard drive for archiving—leaving all your files on the disk. If you can afford it, I recommend getting a tape drive. The cheaper versions of these are not expensive, although they can be slow in both the backing up and formatting of the tape.

Current work, housekeeping and archiving, require different approaches to file organization. If you want a file to be part of your current work, you need to be able to open the application and the file as quickly as possible. You probably don't need to move it around. Housekeeping requires you to be able to be able to select files quickly, and also display the destination disk and directory of any file you move. Finally, in order to archive you need to select groups of files and move them to a disk or tape.

How do you decide into which group any particular file falls? You may divide files into current work and archivable files. Since housekeeping can affect any kind of file, it makes sense to arrange Windows to fit. The best way to keep current work is by the use of file icons in Program Manager. Do your housekeeping in File Manager, and use a backup program to store archivable files.

File icons—OK in small doses

In a perfect world, how would you like Windows to arrange your files? If you've had any experience with Apple's Macintosh you'll know that this computer creates a file icon when you save a file, and double-clicking on the file icon opens the file in the application in which it was created. This sounds like the perfect solution, but in practice creates problems.

Since the Mac makes an icon for every file, its windows soon become clogged with dozens of icons which often obscure the application icon (the Mac doesn't easily distinguish between program and file icons). You can't delete any of these icons, because you'll also delete the files. Smarter Mac users sort their file icons into new directories (the Mac calls them *folders*), but it's still a lot to manage.

Were this scheme available in Windows, managing the icons would be more difficult. The Mac conceals many of the system and application files,where Windows shows you every file DOS handles. My computer has over 8,000 files on it (I'm not that productive, the great majority were installed with programs), but imagine trying to zero in on the file you want among 7,999 similar icons! Program Manager won't allow this, it has a limit of 40 windows and 50 icons per window.

Now, before you rush out to sell your Windows computer and buy a Mac, think about what you really need to access. Current work usually consists of only a handful of files. It would be nice to have every recent file as an icon, but the computer can't tell what's *recent*, so the window is soon congested.

Would you settle for around a half dozen icons you could double-click on and start to work on the files? There's no reason why you can't have more, but what's the point of having icons you'll never use? After all, you may double-click on an entry in File Manager to start up the program and the file, so it makes sense to limit your Program Manager icons to just works in progress.

File icons with long names

There's another benefit to file icons. Apple ads mock the fact that Windows users must use DOS name conventions; why call a file TYLETKAT.TXT when you can call it Thank You Letter to Katherine. In that case, Mac users should hope that Katherine is single, because Windows file icons allow you up to 40 letters and spaces as apposed to the Mac's 32. Unassisted Windows 3.1 will let you describe a file as Thank You Letter to Katherine and Jerry, and arrange it neatly in four lines. The Mac puts all its names on one line—anything over about sixteen characters runs into the icon next to it.

Recall that I stated Windows will let you describe a file. Unfortunately, the file must still be called TYLETKAT.TXT when you save it—that's its DOS name. However, Windows lets you use a long description for any icon, and as long as you include the DOS name of the file in its properties, you may describe the file as you wish. After all, the icon called File Manager is called WINFILE.EXE in the program.

Because setting up file icons isn't automatic, it makes sense not create one for every file. You'll also probably want to keep your file icons in a window separate from your applications, and you don't want to fill this with icons. (If you really need instant access to dozens of files, you should use the launcher that comes with programs such as PC Tools for Windows. See chapter 10.)

Making File Icons

The first thing you need to do is create a window for your file icons. Although one may be sufficient, perhaps you'd work better with several windows, arranged by client or project. To do this, execute the following steps:

   1. Go to **New** on Program Manager's File menu, and select **Group.**

2. Call this **Files,** unless you're making several windows.

3. Repeat steps one and two to create more windows, if necessary.

Creating file icons is a two-stage process; first you create the icon, then you give it a description. There are two ways of creating a file icon; the quicker way requires you to remember the path to the file, the longer does this automatically. If you're at home typing things such as C:\WINWORD\PERSONAL\TYLETKAT.DOC, use the quick way. For those who don't like this idea, I'll start with the slower method.

The slower (but easier) method is as follows:

1. In Program Manager, open the **Main** window and use the **Maximize** button (located in the top right corner of the screen) to make the window fill the screen, as in figure 7-1 following.

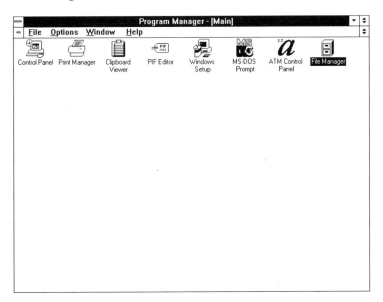

Figure 7-1. Opening the Main window to maximum.

2. Open **File Manager.**

3. Use the **Resize** button to resize File Manager so that Program Manager's Main window is visible behind it, as in figure 7-2 following.

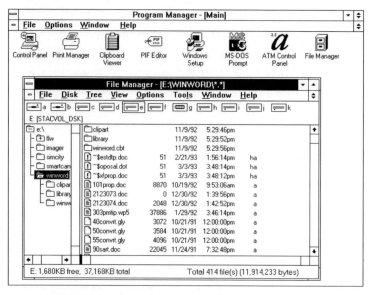

Figure 7-2. File Manager on top of Program Manager.

4. In File Manager, go to the directory of the file you want and scroll if necessary to view details of the tile on the screen.

5. Drag the file icon from File Manager into Program Manager (as in figure 7-3) following. It will automatically create a larger icon with its DOS name.

6. Repeat steps four and five to create the needed file icons. They don't have to be from the same directory or use the same application.

7. Close **File Manager.**

8. **Resize** the **Main** window.

9. Drag the icons into the appropriate file window, as in figure 7-4 below.

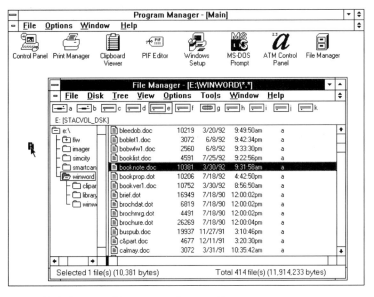

Figure 7-3. Dragging file icons into Program Manager.

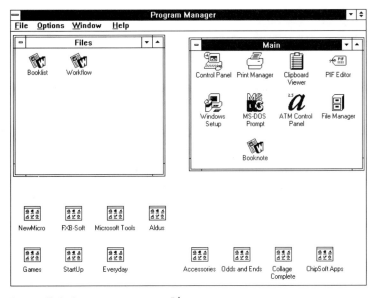

Figure 7-4. Dragging icons into a File group.

Adding a long name

Now assign the icon a description more informative than its DOS filename.

1. Highlight the file icon with a single click. A double-click will open the program and the file, and you don't want to do this just yet.

2. Choose **Properties** on Program Manager's File menu, as shown in figure 7-5 following.

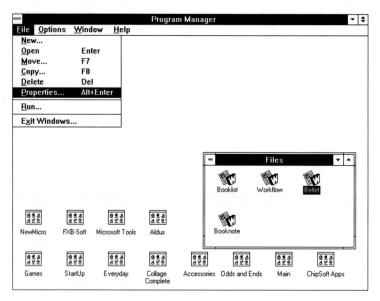

Figure 7-5. The Properties command in Program Manager's File menu.

3. In the top box, marked **Description,** enter a name of up to forty characters or spaces. This could be something like Thank You Letter to Katherine. In the following figure 7-6 I've used Letter to Betty about Visit.

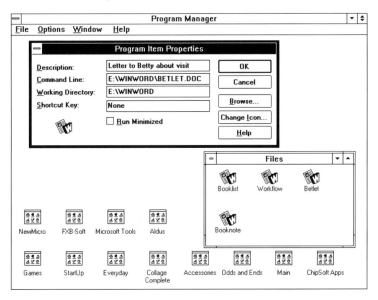

Figure 7-6. Entering a description in the Properties dialog box.

4. Click **OK,** and the file icon will have a new description, as in figure 7-7 following.

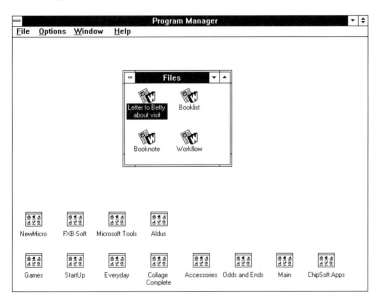

Figure 7-7. A File icon with a long description.

145

The faster (but more complex) method

If you want to type a path to your file, the whole process is much easier. This assumes that the file is associated (linked to a program). To determine if this is true, check to see if the icon in File Manager has several horizontal lines across it. If the icon has no lines inside it, it's not associated. You may create file icons for unassociated files, but it's usually easier to associate them. The discussion on associating files follows this section.

Once you've made a window for your files, hold down the **Control** key and drag any icon into the window. You'll be better off dragging the icon for the application which created your file. At this point you've copied the icon, so you can ignore the entire section which deals with dragging icons from File Manager into Program Manager. Now you need to retrieve the correct path, the correct icon (if necessary), and the correct description.

1. As before, highlight the icon with a single click.

2. Choose **Properties** on Program Manager's File Menu.

3. In the top box marked **Description,** enter up to forty characters or spaces.

4. In the box beneath it, marked Command Line, enter the path to the file so that it reads something like C:\WINWORD\TYLETKAT.DOC.

5. If the icon is incorrect, go to the **Change Icon** button, and use the **Browse** button to locate the executable file, as in figure 7-8 following; here you'll find the icon. Click **OK** to return to the Program Items Properties dialog box.

6. Now click **OK,** and your file icon will be correct.

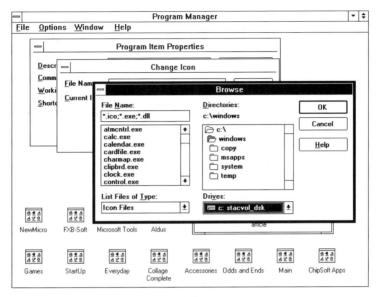

Figure 7-8. Locating a new icon using Browse.

As you can see, you have to follow the instructions for this method to work. Although, this is an easy way to get a new icon from the same directory. Let's suppose you have already made the icon of Thank you Letter to Katherine.

1. Copy the file icon by **Control-dragging.**

2. Choose **Properties** as before.

3. Give the icon a new description as before. If you wrote another thank you letter, this time to Jerry, it could be Thank You Letter to Jerry, so you can highlight Katherine's name only and change just that.

4. In the **Command Line box,** change only the name of the file, the TYLETKAT part, to reflect the new filename. This time you will end up with something such as C:\WINWORD\TYLETJER.DOC.

5. Click **OK,** and your icon will be correct.

147

Using the DOS Path

If you understand anything about a DOS path, you'll know that if you ask DOS to run a program or a file, it will search for it in the directory you give. If it's not there, DOS looks in all the directories mentioned in the PATH statement in your AUTOEXEC.BAT file. Word for Windows automatically puts its name and location in the PATH statement, so you could shorten the Command Line entry above to TYLETJER.DOC, without the C:\WINWORD path before it. Don't try this until you're certain that there's a reference in your PATH statement to the directory that contains your file.

The advantage of this method is that if you decide to move Word for Windows to another drive or partition, the only thing that needs to be altered is the path statement. If you put the path in the Command Line section, you'd have to alter each icon's properties. By the way, if you do move a program to another drive, always reinstall it and then delete the original. Windows keeps information on programs in several different places, and reinstalling is the only way to be certain that all those files are up to date.

You'll probably agree now that, even creating icons the most painless way, it's not something you'd like to do many times over. Unless you're dedicated, you're unlikely to have dozens of file icons. But what happens when your current work is completed, and you don't need the file icon? Just delete it, using the Delete command in Program Manager's File menu; remember, you can't delete the file, except from File Manager.

File Icon Tips and Tricks

There are plenty of twists to making file icons. Let's suppose you've used Ami Pro and Paradox to make files for a particular client, and this pattern of work is likely to continue. You may **Control-drag** the Ami and Paradox icons into the window to copy them, so that you now have everything you need in order to deal with that client located in one window. You may create any number of file icons for the same file.

You may also use Windows' extended characters (the ones you can't find on the keyboard). However, only some of these work—try some and see. Access these characters by holding down the **Alt** key and typing in a four-digit number on the numeric keyboard. See table 4.1 for some examples (You must use the **Alt-key** method here. There's a better method for getting these characters in applications which is described in chapters eight and nine following.)

If you have files from an application which you need to distinguish from other files with the same icon, you may change the icon library MORICONS.DLL or PROGMAN.EXE for example, using the **Change Icon** button in the Properties dialog box. MORICONS.DLL and PROGMAN.EXE are in your Windows directory.

Associating Files with Applications

As you navigate around File Manager, notice that files have different icons. There are gray boxes with blue tops which denote executable files. Most files have an open *page* icon with the corner turned over. Some files have a similar icon, but with horizontal lines. The lines mean that these files are associated with an application, as shown in figure 7-9 following.

If you double-click on associated files in File Manager, the application and file open. Associations are created automatically when you install programs, but you can also set them up manually from File Manager's File menu, using the **Associate** command. Type the three-letter extension and choose the application you want to associate with it. You can't use DOS wildcards in the extension.

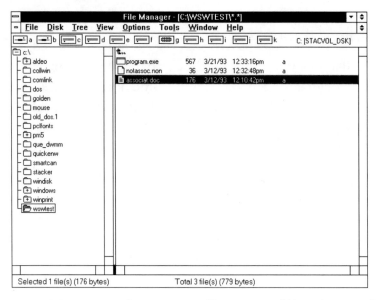

Figure 7-9. From top to bottom; program file, unassociated file, and associated file.

Association tips and tricks

Associating isn't a one-to-one command; you can associate more than one extension with a program. Suppose for example, you have Word for Windows installed on your computer. When you installed it, the program told Windows that all files ending in .DOC were Word for Windows files, and to open Word for Windows whenever you double-clicked on a .DOC file in File Manager.

You may have upgraded from WordPerfect, and had many files which ended in .WP5. You may have removed WordPerfect for DOS because you know that Word for Windows can read files created in WordPerfect format, but if you like to launch files from File Manager you can't do this with the WordPerfect files, because they don't have an association.

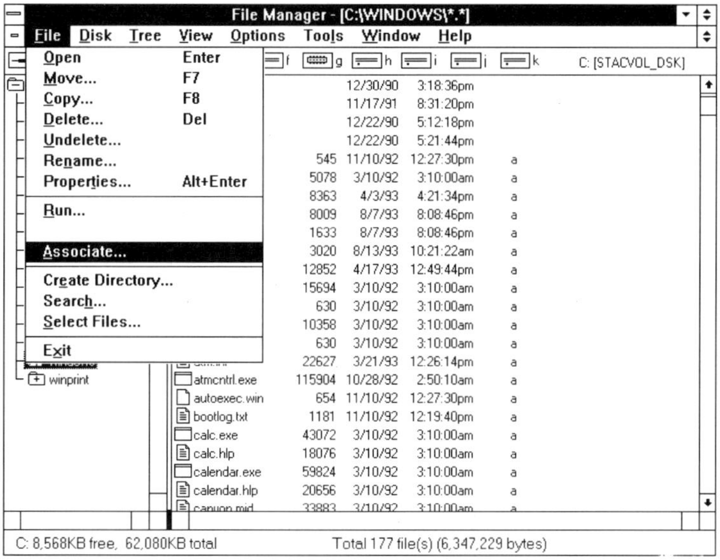

File Manager - [C:\WINDOWS*.*]

File Disk Tree View Options Tools Window Help

Open	Enter		C: [STACVOL_DSK]
Move...	F7	12/30/90	3:18:36pm
Copy...	F8	11/17/91	8:31:20pm
Delete...	Del	12/22/90	5:12:18pm
Undelete...		12/22/90	5:21:44pm
Rename...		545 11/10/92	12:27:30pm a
Properties...	Alt+Enter	5078 3/10/92	3:10:00am a
		8363 4/3/93	4:21:34pm a
Run...		8009 8/7/93	8:08:46pm a
		1633 8/7/93	8:08:46pm a
Associate...		3020 8/13/93	10:21:22am a
		12852 4/17/93	12:49:44pm a
Create Directory...		15694 3/10/92	3:10:00am a
Search...		630 3/10/92	3:10:00am a
Select Files...		10358 3/10/92	3:10:00am a
		630 3/10/92	3:10:00am a
Exit		22627 3/21/93	12:26:14pm a

winprint
atmcntrl.exe   115904   10/28/92   2:50:10am   a
autoexec.win   654   11/10/92   12:27:30pm   a
bootlog.txt   1181   11/10/92   12:19:40pm   a
calc.exe   43072   3/10/92   3:10:00am   a
calc.hlp   18076   3/10/92   3:10:00am   a
calendar.exe   59824   3/10/92   3:10:00am   a
calendar.hlp   20656   3/10/92   3:10:00am   a
canyon.mid   33883   3/10/92   3:10:00am   a

C: 8,568KB free, 62,080KB total   Total 177 file(s) (6,347,229 bytes)

Figure 7-10. File Manager's Associate command.

All you need do is go to the **Associate** command in File Manager, as described in the previous figure 7-10, and enter **.WP5** for the extension. Now, tell Windows to associate all files with this extension with Word for Windows, and double-click on the icon in File Manager to open Word for Windows. You'll have to tell Word for Windows that this is a WordPerfect file, but this system is preferable to looking for WordPerfect files in the Word for Windows Open dialog box.

You need not have files with a particular extension on your computer, and don't have to install the creating applications. If you receive files from other people who use Ami Pro (.SAM) or other WordPerfect extensions such as .WP or .LET, you may add these to your associations. Then, if someone gives you a diskette with their files, you may go to File Manager, select the A or B drive, and immediately open the files with a double-click.

Another good use for extensions is when you have a large number of graphics file formats. Corel Draw, for instance, can read many formats. Its only association is with .CDR, its proprietary format. By

151

associating .BMP, .EPS, .GIF, .TIF, .WMF and other graphics formats with Corel, you can quickly take a look at an image.

Finally, if you're a Windows hacker, you'll have come across some of the many .BAT and .COM files which start applications. I associate .BAT and .COM with Windows Notepad, so that I can see what's inside the file (If you don't understand .BAT and .COM files, leave them alone; you'll foul up your applications if you alter these files without knowing what you're doing).

It's possible to make a file icon in Program Manager without the file being associated with an application. To do so, enter something such as C:\WINWORD\WINWORD.EXE D:\WP5\RESUME.WP5 in the **Command Line box** in the Program Item Properties dialog box. This comprises the path to the executable file, one space, and the path to the data file, if the data file is in a different directory (if it's in the same directory, just put in the name and extension). You may even let one program open data files associated with another with this method. Although these tips can be useful, it's far easier just to associate files.

Exploiting the StartUp Group

Windows has an underused ability; it may start-up any program as soon as you begin a Windows session. Now that you know how to make file icons, you can make Windows start them as well. All you need do is drag the file icon into the StartUp group; it will open as soon as you open Windows.

This is great if you're working late and don't have time to finish what you're doing. Save what you've done and move the icon into the StartUp group. You won't forget this in the morning. If you have to ask someone else to finish it off, they won't need to look for it. If you don't want the file to open your next session, just drag it out of StartUp into another group. In later chapters, you'll see how to use StartUp to keep useful programs a couple of key-clicks away.

Improving a Desktop

Clock is a very useful Windows accessory; it may be set to automatically show the time and date in any application. To do this, you'll need to take advantage of StartUp.

1. Drag the **Clock** icon into the **StartUp** group.

2. Double-click on the icon to open the clock window.

3. Choose settings to suit your taste. I choose Digital, with Seconds and Date.

4. Reduce the window to about an inch and a half in width and half an inch in height. Don't worry if you can't see the details.

5. Move the window to a point just to the left of the minimize button in the Program Manager window.

6. Click on the **Control Button** (the one in the top left of the window, with the horizontal bar across it).

7. From the resulting drop-down menu, choose **Always on Top.**

8. Finally, choose **No Title** from the settings menu.

You now have a box with a gray background, which displays the time and date. As you increase or decrease the size of the box, the numbers will adjust accordingly. In order to get the Settings menu back double-click inside the box, and it will appear again.

In future, since the icon is in the StartUp group, it will run every time you open Windows. Since you selected Always on Top, that's where the icon will appear in every application. Obviously, if your system clock is incorrect, this box won't be worthwhile. You need to adjust the time and date in the Control Panel to the current time. This provides the added bonus of giving your files a correct time and date when they are saved. Your system clock will probably run fast or slow–you should check it regularly.

Changing Clock's settings

You may be tempted to use the Set Fonts command. Although this allows you to use any font on your system for the clock, the space between characters in most fonts is optimized for text. As a result, the figures in the date can be difficult to read because they are too close to the slashes. I'd leave this command alone, or choose fonts such as FixedSys, System, or fonts whose name begins with MS.

Some people prefer an analog clock, even though this means you can't see the date, and the window needs to be greater than half an inch high to show the time clearly. Once this window is larger it usually obscures something important in an application. You may move the Clock window, if it gets in the way; it will open a new session in the same place in which you left it.

8

How Windows Accessories can Speed your Work

Windows 3.1 contains twelve *applets*. These are utility and small programs which are limited versions of common application types. Some programs are included with the package, so that program manufacturers know there is a word processor for their Read Me files. Other programs are included in order to demonstrate what a full-featured version can do while some are a useful reference tool when you're using another program. Since some of these programs are discussed in the next chapter, I'll save the best for last.

Write

Windows Write is a word processor which doesn't compare favorably with full-feature products. Although it has some of the abilities of more expensive word processors, it lacks a dictionary and, consequently, the ability to spell-check. This probably isn't a significant disability since Word for Windows dictionaries consume around one and a half megabytes of memory, and this would have been added to every Windows installation.

Write may be useful to knock out a quick memo, but most people use one of the major Windows word processors. I use it mainly for reading .INI files. The search command in Write can show you the references to a particular program or feature. Often, if there's a file I can't decipher from its extension, I'll try reading it in Write.

One warning about Write. If you use it to edit files such as AUTOEXEC.BAT, you may be misled by Write's limited features and assume it automatically saves files in ASCII format. Write has its own format, and DOS rejects the spurious characters that are part of AUTOEXEC.BAT, if you save it in Write's default format.

Notepad

If Write is a slimmed-down version of a *real* word processor, then Notepad is positively anemic. Microsoft calls it a text editor as opposed to a word processor, and suggests you use it to edit system files. Notepad can't open files larger than about 50 kilobytes, and saves and opens only in ASCII format. This is why Microsoft recommends it for editing system files, since there are no spurious formatting characters in the file.

One feature of Notepad allows you to use the program as a log; this feature doesn't appear to exist in any similar program. Open a new file, and type .LOG. Add any comments you want (or none) and save the file. Each time you open the file, Notepad inserts the time and date. You're then free to add more comments. You may also press **F5** at any time to insert the time and date. Take a look at figure 8-1 following.

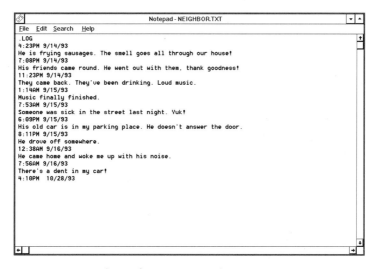

Figure 8-1. Using the Log feature in Notepad.

Object Packager

Object Packager appears to be a cumbersome program which does something you don't actually need a program to do. This is nearly true. Object Packager allows you to embed icons into documents, so that double-clicking on the icon opens a program or a file.

You may do this more simply by opening the document in which you want to insert icons, open File Manager, and then drag the file icon out of File manager into the open document window. The icon positions itself at the cursor position, but may be treated as a graphic and dragged to a new position in the document. This may be all you need, but if you want longer file names you'll need to use Object Packager.

You may be familiar with the procedure of dragging icons out of File Manager, (and into a Program Manager group) from the method discussed earlier to create file icons. The second part of that process involved using Properties to give the icon a long name–up to forty characters.

When you place an icon in an open document, it takes its DOS name and extension, so that the icon appears with a document name such as JILLMEMO.DOC. Once in the document, the icon is impossible to edit. You may move the icon from File Manager to a Program Manager group and then give it a long name, but once you've done this you can't move it into a document. As a result, your embedded icons must have a DOS name, so you end up with a not very elegant document resembling Figure 8-2 following.

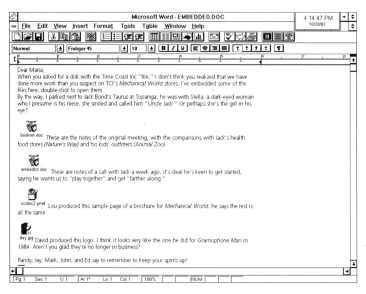

Figure 8-2. Files embedded in a document using drag and drop.

However, if you use Object Packager, it has a command under its Edit menu entitled **Label,** which allows you to give the icons longer names. To reach this point, you'll have to open Object Packager, click in the **Content** window, and select **Import** from the

File menu. You'll observe a dialog box similar to the one you see when you open a file. Pick your file, choose **OK,** and the name will appear in the *Content* window as the icon appears in the **Appearance** window. At this point, you may choose a new name for the file using **Label.** You may also change the icon by pressing the **Insert Icon** button. If you look at figure 8-4 you'll notice the document is the same as in the previous figure 8-2, but this time the icons have long file names.

When you've changed the label and icon to your satisfaction, place the icon in an application by the copy and paste method. Select **Copy Package** from the Edit menu, and then move to the application in which you want the file to be embedded. Place the cursor at the point at which you want the icon to appear, and choose **Paste** from the application's Edit menu. At that point the icon will appear, double-click on it to open the document.

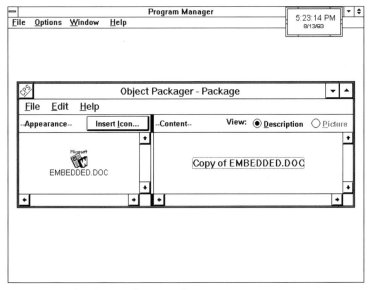

Figure 8-3. The Object Packager Window.

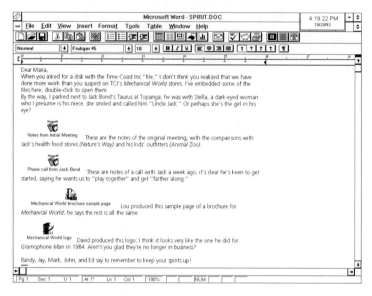

Figure 8-4. Files embedded in a document using Object Packager.

Each document embed in a file becomes a part of that file. You could save the file as a master document, with the embedded document just a mouse-click away. The alternative to the message in figures 8-2 and 8-4 would be to give someone a diskette with a paper message attached to it. By using this process the recipient sees only one file on the disk, and reads the instructions once that file is opened. Of course, the recipient must have the applications which created the embedded files.

Incidentally, Microsoft doesn't regard Object Packager as one of the applets, although it puts the icon in the Accessories group.

Media Player

This feature is part of the multimedia extensions introduced in Windows 3.1.

160

Clock

Clock was covered in the previous chapter.

Sound Recorder

This feature is also part of the multimedia extensions introduced in Windows 3.1.

Recorder

In theory, Recorder should be one of the best tools available from the Windows Accessories. In fact, for a variety of reasons, it's never quite made it to that position.

Recorder enables you to create macros. Macros are a series of operations which can be run using only one keystroke. If you're accustomed to DOS, you'll know about batch files, which execute a number of instructions from a single command. The best-known of these is AUTOEXEC.BAT. Even if you're not interested in DOS, you evoke many commands when you type WIN at the DOS prompt. Similarly, macros work by chaining commands together.

From the demonstrations of macros that I've seen, they vary from the mundane to the spectacular. Yet, they all have one thing in common; no one seems to know how to use them to increase productivity. This is probably because many applications have their own automation, and Windows itself doesn't have repetitive keystrokes that can be combined into one. There are ways of working (particularly in File Manager) that may lead to many repetitive actions. However these may be avoided by using actions such as sorting and displaying only certain types of file.

Later in this book, I cover productivity within applications, but you should be aware of tools such as styles, master pages, glossaries, and application macros, as well as the intelligent use of cut-and-paste and search-and-replace.

161

You may have wondered why Windows always permits you to carry out actions using keyboard commands, when a mouse is a better tool for many tasks. The answer is that you can incorporate these keyboard commands into macros. Although Recorder can incorporate mouse movements into macros as well, this assumes that the macro is run on a single machine where the windows are located in the same place each time, since the program records screen coordinates.

There are commercial programs that do what Recorder does, but do it better. For instance, once you create a macro in Recorder, you can't edit it. However, the best way of automating your work with macro-like actions is to use the scripting languages which are provided by programs such as PC Tools and Norton Desktop. Just using the desktop in these programs speeds up your work faster than any macro.

Paintbrush

Paintbrush is an entry-level paint program, but has one or two surprising strengths. Much of the reason for its existence in Windows was that Microsoft wanted a colorful application available. Paintbrush is the successor to Microsoft Paint, which was bundled with versions of Windows before version 3.0.

Paint programs have almost ceased to exist, with one big exception—photo editing programs—for general illustrations, a draw program is preferable. Since Micrografx Windows Draw retails for well under $100, and Corel Draw 3 sells for less than $200, it's easy to move up from Paintbrush.

A paint program differs from a draw program because it has a file that consists of color values for every pixel on the screen. Consequently everything you paint has dimensions measured in whole pixels–currently 96 pixels to the inch on VGA screens. If you complain about jagged edges on artwork reproduced on 300 dots per inch printers, imagine 96 dots to the inch!

Paint programs can't work with objects, as draw programs can. If you cut-and-paste part of a paint image, you'll leave a white area behind, and the pasted part of the image obliterates whatever it covers—you'll never get it back.

In contrast, draw images consist of objects. The files are not pixel representations, but lists of data which describe the location of an object and its outline. If you move the object, you change its location data in the image. Objects can overlap and stack, and the outlines can be as smooth as the screen or printer which images them.

Paintbrush takes some mastering if you haven't had much experience with a graphics program. Icons in the Toolbox make sense after you've used the program for sometime, but they are confusing to the newcomer. There's also the problem of learning new concepts such as Image Attributes and Pels.

If you stick to the basics, you can create simple graphic objects such as triangles, for instance, and place or embed them into your page layout program. Paintbrush saves in either .BMP or .PCX format; don't save in formats that have a greater number of colors than you need.

If you own Microsoft Word for Windows, it is sold with Microsoft Draw, a basic draw program (as opposed to a paint program). You may access it by clicking on the Draw icon (a gray circle, a black triangle, and a white square). You may embed drawings using cut and paste. Microsoft Draw can't be used except as part of another Microsoft program.

Terminal

This is a simple communications program, which may prove useful if your modem has no Windows software. However the lack of features doesn't make this a significant product, especially since full-fledged communications packages cost less than $100 retail.

If you *visit* few bulletin boards and don't download many files, you may find that Terminal is sufficient. The downloading protocols are limited to two, instead of the ten or more you'll find on the free software sold along with the modem. There's no dialing directory, and you have to load a DOS file each time to access different bulletin boards.

Calendar and Cardfile

I deal with these two applets together, because they are usually combined in commercial products called PIMs (Personal Information Managers). Calendar keeps track of your appointments, while Cardfile maintains an address list. Compared to some of the applets in Windows, these two programs have more of the features you'd hope for, though they're still no competition for commercial products.

Calendar gives you a day view, with appointments listed either every hour, half-hour, or quarter-hour. You may also see a month view, and the program allows you to view months in the past or future. You may assign an alarm for particular appointments, use a visual alarm and also make your computer beep. You may also mark special days on the monthly calendar; in the Windows documentation, Microsoft provides a list, starting with the most important—Payday.

Cardfile is similar to a Rolodex list of names and addresses. You may enter specific details such as a name on the index line (of up to 39 characters), and then enter the address on the rest of the card. Cardfile can be used for names and addresses as well as recipes, since Cardfile permits you to have multiple files. You may have any mix you want—names, recipes, or any other files you want to keep.

A significant drawback of Cardfile is that there's no easy way of sorting files, other than alphabetically by first characters or by text on the index line. If you create an index line that says Joe Blow—

BigCo, Inc., if you search on BigCo all these records are brought to the front (see figure 8-5 for an example). If you wanted to pick up all the names in Anytown, unless you'd put the city in the index line, you would have to use the Search command. This wouldn't sort the cards, but just display them, one by one. Similarly, if you had recipes and wanted to use one containing oregano, you couldn't bring the cards together.

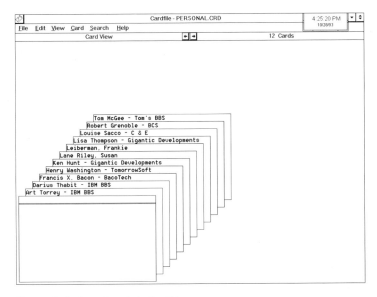

Figure 8-5. Sorted cards in Cardfile.

However, one nifty trick of Cardfile is its ability to dial a number. If you have a telephone number anywhere on the card, and a Hayes-compatible modem (almost all modems are Hayes-compatible), all you need do is select the card; choosing autodial does the rest. You can also print the cards, and even use Paintbrush to put illustrations on them.

For casual use, Calendar and Cardfile may satisfy you, but some commercial PIMs like Lotus Organizer sell for around $100, and offer sufficiently more than the Windows applets to make them a worthwhile investment.

Calculator

Although there are more fully-featured commercial products than Calculator, most of the jobs for which you need a calculator are very basic. That's why I suggest you keep Calculator handy—the next chapter shows you how—because you'll probably use it regularly.

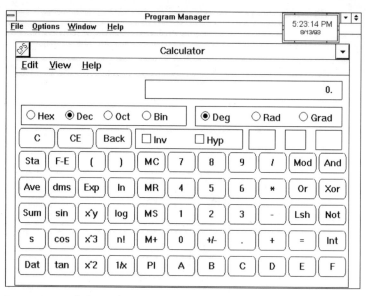

Figure 8-6. Calculator, shown in scientific mode.

Calculator has two faces; it's a basic, four-function machine, and also a scientific calculator, as shown in figure 8-6 previously. Calculator scores over conventional calculators because it can't get lost under your papers on your desk, and you may cut and paste numbers to and from it on your computer screen.

When your computer has Num Lock on (which is usually the case) you may use the numeric keypad and the Enter key for equals. The slash key (/) is divide, and the asterisk (*) is multiply.

If you're using an application, for example a word processor, and you want to perform a mathematical operation on a number you've just typed, copy it to the clip board, go to Calculator (I'll show how to do this fastest in the next chapter), and paste in the number. Now perform the calculations, copy the answer to the clip board, return to the word processor, and paste the number at the appropriate point.

If you go to **View,** you may choose the scientific calculator. This calculator has the usual range of scientific functions, including statistical, number-base, and trigonometric calculations. Naturally, you may display numbers exponentially. If you don't understand what the scientific functions are for, you won't get a lesson from the documentation or the help files. For example, you need to know what a standard deviation is in order, to use this calculator.

In as much as a calculator using the power of a computer with the display of a monitor could run rings around a hand-held unit, it's clear that Microsoft wanted to reassure users rather than extend their reach. Some of the commercially-equivalent products such as the one in Norton Desktop, have a very useful "tape" calculator, which displays every step of a calculation. However, because most of the time you need simple arithmetic, Calculator may fit the bill.

Character Map

This is probably the most useful of all the applets after Clock, yet most people don't know it exists. It is available, in stripped-down form, as a built-in feature in Word for Windows (as Symbol on the Insert menu), where it displays all the characters available in the symbol fonts. Other programs have a similar feature, but most don't. Character Map shows you every character you may use in any font; not just the symbol fonts. It allows you to copy and paste them into an application, and is displayed in the following figure 8-7.

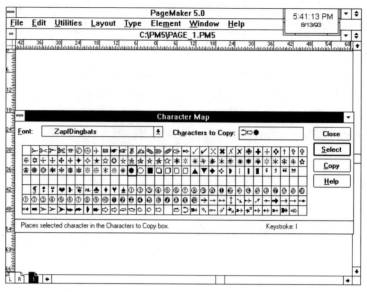

Figure 8-7. Character Map.

You may not be aware that there are over two hundred characters in most fonts, and only half of which may be accessed with normal keyboard commands. Many of these are accented characters, but there are also bullets, a few fractions, correct (curved) quotation marks, apostrophes, currency symbols, and more.

You also need to view characters in symbol fonts; Windows 3.1 comes with Wingdings and Symbol, as well as several others, like Zapf Dingbats. All of these characters may be accessed by holding down the **Alt** key and entering a four-digit number on the numeric keypad.

The problem arises when you want to use one of these special characters. I can remember the code for a few; **Alt-189** gives you a true half character ($\frac{1}{2}$), which looks far better than typing 1/2. **Alt-0151** provides an **Em** dash, and **Alt-145** through **Alt-148** yields correct quote marks. When it comes to Symbol and Wingding fonts, I can't remember the codes for any of the characters.

Many use one of the charts which come with different applications and then promptly lose them. You may have a book that lists the Alt key combinations; do you know where it is now, and which page lists the key commands?

Character Map is the answer to this. If you need a special character, you can open this application, and display in a grid all characters in the font. If you click on any character, it displays at double size, and you will see the Alt key combination necessary to create the character.

However, you don't need to use the Alt combination. You can select a character with the mouse and press the Select button; it will appear in the **Characters to Copy** window. Click on the **Copy** button and the character is copied to the clipboard. Return to your application, and paste the character in the position you want.

When you're in Character Map, you may select any font on your system to see which characters it contains. You may choose more than one character to **Select.** When you press **Copy,** they'll all be copied to the clipboard. Of course, you can paste the character as often as your document requires it. You may browse the rest of the character set in a normal font, and find what's in those symbol fonts. You may also have ornament fonts as well; Character Map shows you the ornaments and the keystroke needed to reach them.

If you've never used special characters, this may sound trivial, but when you need a particular symbol, there's no better method to access it. One day you will need to find a British Pound Sterling symbol; unless you know that it's available as **Alt-0163,** you will simply end up typing L15,000, as opposed to £15,000.

Even if you do know that the character exists, you probably don't know the code. Although some books describe these codes, it's impossible to remember which books and what pages. There are charts; you'll lose them. One book I purchased supplied a mouse pad with a transparent top and a chart that mounted under the pad;

this was fine, except that I couldn't read the codes because the type was too small.

It's quite possible to waste half an hour desperately trying to find something that tells you what keys to press, or to waste space with a chart taped to the wall by your computer. Even if you can lay hands on this information, it's only good for one or two fonts.

It's especially sad to see so many desktop published documents with straight quotes—the hallmark of the beginner. Although more and more DTP programs convert the quotes you enter into curly quotes, there are enough desktop publishers out there who have no idea how to get this right. Character Map provides you with this information immediately.

At this point, you may be thinking, "these applets sound like they could be useful, but I don't want to have to quit my application to use them."

You don't have to.

In the next chapter I'll explain how you may run several applications at once and switch between them instantly.

9

Unleashing the Power of Multitasking

In the 1940s and 1950s, when computers were young, they were only used to carry out one computation at a time. The 1960s saw the proliferation of business computers, and the introduction of a new term: data processing. Unlike the scientific and mathematical calculations of the previous decade, business computing was more concerned with moving data. Math requirements were minimal, but information had to be available to many users.

Computer scientists responded by devising systems comprised of many screens and keyboards (called terminals) that were connected to one processor. Software controlled input from, and output to, the terminals, while making the processor available to each active terminal in rotation. Although other terminals had to wait their turn, the wait was so brief that each user appeared to have full use of the processor. Even in the 1960s and 1970s, the processor was sufficiently powerful, so much so that the computer spent most of its time waiting to input or output.

During the 1980s, machines that looked very much like terminals appeared in businesses. These new machines contained their own processors and disk storage. They were called personal computers.

171

Although many personal computers are now connected to networks for sharing files and printers, the processor of each unit is fully adequate for computation.

You may run Windows on a personal computer, but only one person may use it at a time. This isn't exactly a drawback. Personal computers cost around two thousand dollars, so most businesses buy enough machines to go around. The only computer that may be used by more than one person is a file server on a network, and this machine merely stores files and controls their access.

A Different Kind of Multitasking

It may seem that there is no longer any need for multitasking, since we all have enough power at hand. That's true, but there's another type of multitasking that can pay great dividends. You're probably not even aware of it, particularly if you brought your DOS habits to Windows.

Generally, working with DOS means opening an application, saving the results, closing the application and starting another. This is probably similar to the way you're working with Windows, but you can dramatically improve your productivity by breaking out of the DOS routine. Multitasking means that several programs run at the same time, on the same computer, and are accessed by a single user.

Multitasking in this form began in DOS. In the mid 1980s, a small company named Borland introduced a new kind of program called Terminate and Stay Resident (TSR). Their program, SideKick, had to be started before you opened any other programs. Although it appeared to close, the program remained resident in RAM. When another application was opened, you could revive SideKick with a special keyboard combination, and its features—address book, calendar, and other utilities—became available. Once you'd used SideKick, you could close it and go back to your application. SideKick would remain ready to access whenever you needed it.

Within programs you multitask like this fairly often. If you use a spell checker in a word processing program, the dictionary is loaded into RAM while some of the main program is stored until you've finished checking. Similarly, if you use Windows Help, the Help program and files are loaded into RAM and your application is stored on the hard disk until you're done.

Windows is far more able than DOS to exploit single-user multitasking, though it is still less functional than Windows NT. A fault in any Windows program causes the whole machine to crash, where a more sophisticated operating system simply closes the offending application and carrys on. However, you can still easily make use of Windows multitasking.

Exploiting Windows Multitasking

Multitasking isn't some kind of Windows parlor trick—it has immediate benefits that can improve the way you work every day. These are:

- Access to other programs.

- Access to utilities and housekeeping.

- Using two programs on one document.

Suppose you are busy typing a memo, and you suddenly remember that you need some information from a spreadsheet. If you act as you did in your DOS days, you probably select exit in your word processor, start your spreadsheet, jot down the information, and exit the spreadsheet. Then you start the word processor and type in the figures from the spreadsheet.

With multitasking, you leave the word processor, but don't exit it (I'll explain how shortly). You open the spreadsheet, copy the figures, change back to the word processor, and paste the figures into your document. If you realize that you picked the wrong figures, you can change instantly to your spreadsheet select the correct data, and instantly return to your word processor.

Here's another example. You're finishing a letter when you realize that you have to make a copy of the file on a diskette. None of the diskettes you have is formatted. You could exit your word processor, open File Manager, format the diskette, then reopen your word processor and finish the letter. Then you might go back to File Manager and copy the file from your hard disk to the diskette.

I'll show you how to switch instantly to File Manager, start formatting the diskette, and return to your word processor while the disk is formatting and finish the letter. Then you can save the file to your hard drive and also to the floppy.

Finally, you might be creating a publication in PageMaker, with an illustration from Corel Draw's clip art library. You decide that Corel has another piece of clip art that's even more suitable. You can select exit in PageMaker, open Corel, export the new more suitable image, reopen PageMaker, delete the existing clip art, and import the new image. Whew!

By using multitasking, you can switch to Corel immediately, browse the clip art libraries, export a suitable image, change back to PageMaker, select the existing art, and import the new image to replace it.

What does multitasking let you do?

Without making any alterations to the default Windows set up:

- You can pause your work in one program and open any other program; either program can be a DOS program, so long as you started it in Windows.

- You can return to your original program, and exit the other program, or keep it open.

- You can be at any stage in the program you stop using; dialog boxes can be opened, processes like file downloading or disk formatting can be underway.

- You can cut or copy information in one program and paste it into another, using this method.

With a minimal amount of work:

- You can automatically have several other programs open at all times, and only see them when you need to use them.

- You can have many programs open at once. The number is limited by RAM and virtual memory; you set virtual memory by using Control Panel to make a permanent swap file (you'll see how to do this later in this chapter). However, if you have only four megabytes of RAM, you can still multitask easily.

Of all the techniques outlined in this book, multitasking has the widest use and makes you the most productive.

Cool Working with the Cool Switch

The secret of multitasking is what Microsoft calls the *cool switch*— the **Alt+Tab** combination. To switch between programs, you hold down the **Alt** key and press **Tab** one time to change to another program. You don't see the program itself; but a box in the center of your screen with the program's icon, the program's name, and the name of any file that you're using in the program. Pressing **Tab** will cycle you through all programs that are running. After you change to another program, the first program you see in this way will be the program you switched from last.

There are more ways of seeing other programs that you're running. The Alt+Esc combination displays programs one after another at full screen, unless you've checked **Run Minimized** in their Program

Item Properties dialog box, in which case you'll just see the program's icon (more about this later). You can also press **Ctrl-Esc** to bring up the **Task List;** this is a dialog box with a list of all running programs. You can highlight another program and, either switch to it, or close it. You can also display all non-minimized programs as cascaded or tiled windows. These two methods may be useful on occasion, but they're not as fast as **Alt+Tab.**

Although the Cool Switch is normally functioning, Microsoft provides you with an opportunity to switch it off, presumably to avoid a conflict with a keyboard shortcut in a program. You can test the Cool Switch easily by:

1. In Program Manager's Main window, choose **Control Panel.**

2. In the Control Panel window, choose **Desktop.**

3. In the Applications section, make sure that the **Fast "Alt+Tab" Switching** box is checked.

I checked this point as I wrote this chapter in Word for Windows. I pressed **Alt+Tab** until I saw the box for Program Manager. I followed the instructions above, and memorized the wording in the Desktop dialog box. Then I Alt+Tabbed back to Word for Windows, entered the words Fast Alt+Tab Switching, and then Alt+Tabbed back to the Desktop dialog box to make sure I had the words right. I was glad I did—I'd made a mistake, because I missed the plus sign and the quotes. I corrected the words to read **Fast "Alt+Tab" Switching.**

Whatever program you're running in Windows, Program Manager is also running. This means that you can always Alt+Tab to Program Manager, and from there to any other program you have on your system. As I type this, I still haven't closed the Desktop dialog box. Normally, I'd get a rude beep if I tried to do anything with a dialog box still open, but by using Alt+Tab I can jump to another program with no trouble.

176

Control Panel is a separate Windows program, although it's easy to think of it as part of Program Manager. It has its own filename—CONTROL.EXE. I know this because I just checked it by using Alt+Tab. I skipped the option of going back to Control Panel's Desktop dialog box, and went to Program Manager instead. The Control Panel icon was highlighted, so I went to Properties on the File menu to find Control Panel's DOS name. With the Properties dialog box still open, I Alt+Tabbed back to Word for Windows.

Once you Alt+Tab out of a program, most of the time you can act as if it isn't open. If you try to open a program that only lets you have one version running, Program Manager will tell you that it's *already running*. If you try to use a file you already have open, some programs will say "File [the file's name] already in use by [user's name]. Open a copy?"

However, you won't have to worry about these situations very often. Suppose you have a file you want to back up, but you don't know which backup diskette has enough room. **Alt+Tab** to Program Manager, open **File Manager**, and put your diskettes in the drive, one after the other. Of course, you'll remember to press **F5** whenever you put a new diskette in the drive, to force Program Manager to read the new diskette. When you've found a suitable diskette, just Alt+Tab back to your application and save the file to Drive A or B.

You may have a file on one of several diskettes that you want to use in an application which is already open. Alt+Tab to get to Program Manager and File Manager as before, check each diskette, and either open the file from the diskette or copy it to your hard drive.

Problems with Alt+Tab

There are very few problems with this way of working. There is the slim possibility that your application uses Alt+Tab for something else, or you've set up this key combination to start a macro. Sometimes you can press Tab once too often, and skip the program

177

you meant to switch to. Just keep pressing Tab, and eventually the program will reappear.

Probably the biggest problem is forgetting to use Alt+Tab. I sometimes find myself getting to Program Manager by minimizing my application. Until you get used to the idea that any program is a couple of keystrokes or mouse clicks away, you won't remember to take advantage of this method. Maybe you should write "Alt+Tab" on a post-it and stick it to your monitor.

And forgetting that you're able to Alt+Tab back to the previous application without exiting the program you switched to is often another memory lapse problem. This dumps you back in Program Manager. You can always reopen the application, but it's obviously better to Alt+Tab out of it. Unless you're short of RAM and virtual memory, there's no reason to exit other applications.

You may be worried that you could decide to exit Windows while you still have an application open with an unsaved file. If you use Alt+Tab to return to Program Manager and then choose Exit Windows, you'll see the same dialog box as if you selected Exit within the application.

Getting Set for Better Multitasking

Although you can multitask Windows easily "right out of the box," there are ways to improve the power of your system.

Adding RAM

When you launch Windows programs, they take up part of your RAM. The more programs you run, the more RAM you use, until you're out of RAM. The more RAM you have, the greater your multitasking powers.

Adding RAM is only one way of increasing your memory; there's another method that costs nothing and may have the same effect— it's called virtual memory. This works with any 386 or 486 computer.

Many computers sold in the last few years have four megabytes of RAM which can be expanded to 32. Unless you plan to open several programs at once, four megabytes is sufficient; it lets you run Program Manager, an application, and one or two of the utility programs I will discuss later.

If you plan to run two applications at once, you may choose to add RAM; probably another four megabytes. You may find that memory can only be added to your computer in units of one or four megabytes. A few applications now require eight megabytes of RAM, and no doubt future operating systems will demand more, so RAM you add now won't go to waste.

Virtual Memory

If have a number of programs running under Windows, only one or two are actually doing anything. As I type this, Word for Windows is handling the word processing chores, and Clock is updating the time every second. Program Manager is open and doing nothing.

With virtual memory, programs that are open but not active may be stored on your hard disk. When needed, they can be brought back into RAM, and will display the screen they were using when you last accessed them. This is why you may have the Save dialog box open, in an application and be able to use Alt+Tab to return to Program Manager. Then go to File Manager to check for available disk space. Whether the program is in RAM or on the hard drive, it won't change until you return to it, so the access speed of the storage is not important.

If free space on my RAM was tight, Program Manager could be stored on the hard drive, then swapped into RAM to replace Word for Windows. While I use Program Manager and File Manager, Word

179

for Windows could stay on the hard drive in suspended animation. Then when finished with File Manager, I could swap Word for Windows back into RAM to finish working on my file.

Windows handles this process automatically by using a swap file, which is an area on the hard drive that holds open but inactive programs. Inactive programs are held in RAM if there's room, and swapped to disk if not. You're aware of none of this—Windows will make sure that the programs you select are in RAM when you need them.

A swap file takes up hard disk space, but that's a lot cheaper than buying RAM. There is still loss of speed since information must be loaded to and from disk. Windows has a way to reduce these speed losses to a minimum—it's called a permanent swap file.

The Permanent Swap File

Retrieving information from a disk is slow compared to accessing it from RAM. Your computer has to work out where the information is stored. DOS places information in the first available space on the disk, and if that space can't hold the entire file it stores the remainder somewhere else.

A Windows' Permanent Swap File works around this situation. An area of your hard disk is set aside for program swapping. It's used solely for swapped program files. It's much easier to manage, and Windows doesn't have to look everywhere across the drive to find the files.

The downside of this arrangement is that a small amount—a few megabytes—of your hard drive is not available to other files. If your disk space is limited, this may be a problem. A slightly more annoying difficulty is that you have to set up the file; at least you only have to do once.

You may already have a permanent swap file on your disk. This file may be too big for your needs: This could be because Windows allocated an amount based on the amount of free space on the drive, and this might have happened when Windows was installed onto an almost empty drive. If your computer came with Windows pre-installed, you should check how big your swap file is, and reduce its size if necessary.

Setting Up a Swap File

Swap files require an area of the hard drive that's contiguous (in one unit). If you have a hard drive that's fairly full, you may have a total amount of free space that's actually made up of several smaller areas. So before you create a permanent swap file, it's a good idea to defragment your disk.

You can't place a permanent swap file in drives compressed with many versions of programs like Stacker—check your documentation. You should close all applications except Program Manager. because you don't want any swap file to contain anything when you do this work.

Now you're all set to try the following:

1. From the Main window in Program Manager, open **Control Panel.**

2. Select **386 Enhanced.**

3. In the 386 Enhanced dialog box, select the **Virtual Memory** button.

181

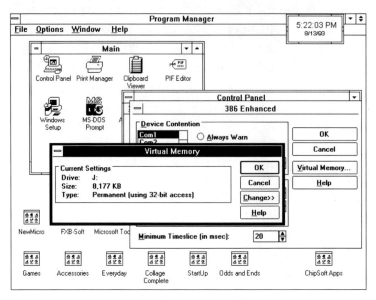

Figure 9-1 Setting up your swap file in Program Manager

You'll see a screen similar to figure 9-1.

I've seen computers with nearly 30 megabytes of virtual memory, which is way too much. This results from setting up Windows when the disk is empty, thus the program allocates around 15 percent of free memory to a swap file. With a 200 megabyte drive, this accounts for the size of the file. This seems unimportant, but as your drive fills this space is wasted.

You may ask, what is the correct size for a permanent swap file? The answer depends on what you wish to store. If what you're trying to store is not just the program, but the program and any file you're working on, you will have to create a swap file big enough to hold this.

My guess is that unless you have large data files—over a megabyte or more—you can manage with a four megabyte swap file. Unless you use image manipulation with programs like Adobe Photoshop or create massive spreadsheets, you're unlikely to have this size of data file. This assumes that you have four megabytes of RAM.

182

My advice is the result of testing applications on my own computer. I find it unlikely that I'd ever have more than three major applications running at the same time. This includes two programs, and a word processor. I have tried opening several applications, and managed to fill up about seven megabytes. Data files vary, but a nine-thousand word chapter of this took up just over 50 kilobytes. A three page newsletter design, with high-resolution photographic illustrations, used a half megabyte in PageMaker.

Getting the Correct Sized Swap File

If you already have the Virtual Memory dialog box open, and you want to change the size of your swap file, simply select the **Change>>** button. You'll see the dialog box shown in figure 9-2.

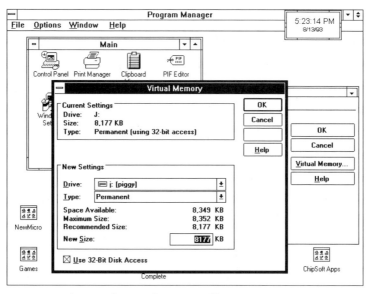

Figure 9-2 Changing the size of your swap file.

Enter the new figure in the space provided, unless this figure is greater than the recommended figure. To get four megabytes, enter 4096; for eight megabytes, enter 8192. These figures don't have to be exact; entering 4000 or 8000 will work just as well, but if you have a figure in whole megabytes it helps to know how much of your hard drive has been taken up.

While you're in the Virtual Memory dialog box, check **Use 32-Bit Disk Access,** if this box is visible or not grayed out, unless you have a portable computer. This will speed your disk accessing if you have a Western Digital-compatible hard drive controller. Most of today's controllers are compatible. Your computer will now access your hard drive direct from Windows, instead of going to DOS.

OKing your way out of this dialog box, will give you the option of restarting Windows or continuing. I'm sure Windows won't let you restart if you have another application open, however I'm happier choosing continue and reaping the benefits of the change in the next session.

Multitasking and the StartUp Group

Although it's easy to Alt+Tab to Program Manager to start the program you need, there's a way to have several programs available at any time, while you're running any application, without even having to select them in Program Manager. In theory, you can have every program available to you with Alt+Tab; in practice, the number depends on the amount of RAM you have and your swap file.

The way to have a program handy is to move or copy the icon into the StartUp group window. Whenever you start a Windows session any program in the StartUp group will also start. Obviously, you don't want them to clutter your screen, and there is a way to prevent this—I'll explain it in a moment. The first thing you must decide, however, is which programs you want to run at all times.

Choosing programs for the StartUp group

Unless you conduct almost all your work in one program, it doesn't make sense to have a major application start up when you start

Windows. The better approach is to choose those programs you'll need to use constantly, like SideKick was in the "old days". SideKick is long gone and its successors are the Personal Information Managers, or PIMs, like PackRat.

While a PIM is a useful program to have running all the time, there are several Windows applets that will be useful to almost everybody. The three I choose are Clock, Calculator, and Character Map. They take up very little RAM but can save you hours of time. You'll have a clock, a basic calculator, and a guide to special characters available immediately.

Depending on the way you work, you could benefit from other applets. You may not need a full-fledged PIM, but prefer to use CardFile and Calendar to store addresses and plan your day. Terminal may satisfy your needs for a communications program, and NotePad could store your to-do list. Since these programs are available to you no matter how many other programs are running, their functionality increases enormously.

There's one other program you should put into StartUp—File Manager. File Manager may well be the program you refer to most of all; whether checking for a file that doesn't appear in the File Open dialog box of your application, looking for space to store a file, or formatting a diskette.

The problem with putting File Manager in the StartUp group is that it doesn't appear in the Main window any more. You can get around this by **Control-dragging** it into StartUp, so that a copy of the icon remains in Main. It doesn't matter how many copies of an icon you make; all it *contains* is the instruction to start the program. You can delete unwanted icons easily by using Program Manager's Delete command from the File menu; all this does is remove the icon—it doesn't affect the program itself.

You may find some icons already in StartUp. These are placed there by programs you've already installed. The software that comes with

185

my WinJet printer card placed an icon in StartUp, and my Microsoft Bookshelf CD-ROM put a Viewer icon there as well. Don't remove or modify any icons you find here.

Making Programs Run Minimized

If you put all the programs you wanted into StartUp and then restarted Windows, you'd get a nasty shock—all the programs would open up on your screen, one after another. You can control this by making each application run as an icon—run minimized. When you Alt+Tab to the application, however, it opens up at full screen.

So before you open Windows with a full StartUp group, make each application run minimized. Here's how.

1. Select an icon.

2. Select **Properties** on Program Manager's File menu.

3. In the Program Item Properties dialog box, check **Run Minimized.**

4. Choose **OK,** and repeat this for every application in the StartUp group.

You may be worried that this might affect the way File Manager will display if you access it from the Main window. It won't make any difference—the properties are being altered for this icon only.

Although the programs are running as icons, when you Alt+Tab they'll open at full screen. Some, like Calculator or Character Map, only occupy part of the screen anyway, so these will appear to "float" over your page.

The Alt+Tab way of life

It takes a certain amount of discipline to remember to use Alt+Tab. It's very easy to slip back into your old ways, especially when programs like Character Map appear over your work with a tempting Close button. Click that button and you're dead! You'll have to Alt+Tab back to the StartUp window and double-click on the icon to get the program running again.

Try to stop yourself from exiting any program, until you're certain that it won't be worth keeping open. You should not leave major applications running—especially if you have sessions where you use a word processor to write letters and memos, and then go on to use a spreadsheet to work out your budget— in instances where there is no overlap. However, desktop publishers, using an illustration program to add a graphic to a publication better keep both programs open until the graphic looks right.

To use Alt+Tab most effectively, you should look at the way you work now. Which programs do you use? Do you find yourself exiting one before you're finished because you have to go to another? Which applets do you use? Answers to these and similar questions will guide you to the most efficient setup.

There are other considerations as well. If you haven't decided to put your name and address list or your day planner on the computer, Alt+Tab may well make this feasible. If someone calls and tells you the date of an upcoming meeting, you may prefer to write it in your day planner, if the alternative is exiting the application you're running, digging the PIM icon out of Program Manager, and starting it. If the PIM icon is in the StartUp group, then it's just a couple of key presses away, and you can leave the PIM program open at the exact place you need.

Remember that you must save any work you want to keep. It's easy to make an image in Corel Draw and cut and paste it into a word processor, and then absent-mindedly say no when the **Do You Want To Save Changes** dialog box appears at the end of your session. Get used to saving anything you want to keep at the time you create it.

Once you start to use Alt+Tab regularly, you'll get a real feeling of power. If you don't have to exit your program to format a diskette or find out how to make a special character, you'll save significant amounts of time. It may only amount to a minute on each occasion, but you could easily use Alt+Tab twenty times a day.

So far, all we've looked at is working in Program Manager and File Manager. Although Windows applications vary widely, they have common traits. Included in these are ways to speed up your work within applications, and many of these are not widely known. In the next chapter, we'll look at them.

10

Speeding Through Windows Applications

In the last few chapters, we've been looking at ways of configuring Windows so that you may work faster. These tips, on their own, will speed you more than resetting any defaults or even making most hardware upgrades. This chapter looks at ways to get around faster within applications.

There are many ways to work faster in Windows applications, but probably the best is to speed through dialog boxes. Any menu item followed by ellipses (...) leads to a dialog box.

To exit most dialog boxes, select either OK or Cancel. You can use the mouse, or do this with Enter (for OK) and Esc (for Cancel). OK means "implement changes (if any)," and Cancel means "act as though this dialog box was never selected". This might seem obvious, but if you want to find your way around an application, you can select any dialog box. Cancel will always get you out of trouble. It's better to select Cancel if you find yourself in a dialog box by mistake. You may have made a change in the settings that doesn't carry over the next time you open the dialog box. In this case, OK can mean "revert to default," which may not be what you need. Also, if you only want to check which printer is selected (in "Print Setup"), clicking OK will make the program read the printer driver again, wasting time.

You may be aware of the quick ways to work in dialog boxes. Tab will move you from one choice to the next. Shift-Tab sends you backwards through the box. Any command in the box which has an underlined character in it can be selected by pressing Alt and the character; if you do this a second time, the choice is unselected. If a name in a box has a downward arrow at its right, this means that there's a drop-down list available if you press the arrow. If the name is highlighted, you can type in a new name. Tab through the dialog box to apply the highlighting to other drop-down lists.

What you may not know is that Windows lets you type in the first letter, and the drop-down box changes to the nearest choice. In PageMaker's Type Specs dialog box, if you type H when the selected font is Times, you'll see Helvetica in the font box. If you select OK, your font will be changed to Helvetica. If you have more than one font beginning with H, press the H key several times to cycle through all your fonts that begin with H.

190

Some applications such as Word for Windows have added to their dialog boxes by providing choices through ribbons and toolbars. These don't let you use Tab to highlight the boxes you want to change. However, you may still use the shortcut of typing the initial letter in Word for Windows version 2. Drag the cursor through the entire font name to highlight it, then type in one or more characters. If you click on the downward arrow, you'll see the nearest choice highlighted. If you click on the down arrow again, that choice will become the new font.

It's possible to make an error in this process by typing in characters which don't apply to any choice in the list; then the original selection remains in place.

I use these tricks constantly. When I want to change to two columns in PageMaker, the dialog box gives me a choice of determining the number of columns and the distance between them. My usual choice with two columns is two picas (a third of an inch) apart. Since you can't make this distance a default, I open the dialog box, type 2-Tab-2, and press enter for OK.

I've already explained how I select fonts in PageMaker. I use the same technique when saving from Word for Windows. Often I must submit articles to people who use Macs, so I save them in the Word 4.0 for Mac format. First, I press F12, for Save As; then tab three times to highlight the save file format. Word has 26 save format options, displayed five at a time; I type W four times and press enter to get the correct one.

You'll notice that I use keyboard rather than mouse commands in most of these tips. If you know what you're doing, they are definitely the quickest way to get the work done. However, I don't use many keyboard shortcuts, since there's always the possibility that you pick the wrong one. It's no fun highlighting an area of text, only to see it disappear since you selected Control-B rather then Control-Shift-B.

So what's the best way to use the keyboard? If you have to use the keyboard to change something in a dialog box, press return instead of reaching twelve inches for the mouse, positioning the cursor over the OK button, and pressing the button.

I often use keyboard shortcuts when I have to make a number of similar changes throughout a document. I use my right hand to move the mouse and select text with both hands on the keyboard to select Control-Shift-I, or whatever combination of keys are necessary. Of course, you should check to see that you can't make these changes globally by using styles or search and replace.

If you've ever worked in WordPerfect for DOS (and many other DOS applications) you'll know the importance of the function keys. Most Windows applications have a full range of commands attached to them. I recently tried the function keys in Word for Windows and discovered what they do. If you want to learn without this "hit or miss" method, look up **Function Keys** under **Keyboard and Mouse** in the Help index.

Of the other keys which are useful in Windows, the chief one must be Shift. In most drawing programs this key gives you perfect squares and circles if you hold it down while selecting the appropriate tool. But do you know its use in word processing and page layout programs?

How many times have you selected one character too many or one too few, when you want to perform some action on the text? You've probably deselected everything, and then had another try. Next time, hold down shift and you'll find you can extend or reduce the area of highlighted text without deselecting everything. You can also highlight one area (or even just place the cursor at one particular point), hold down shift, and then click the cursor in another point. All intervening text will be selected. This even works across pages in page layout programs, and in file lists such as File Manager and dialog boxes.

Perhaps your typing is as poor as mine. You'll view your work in a word processor and see all kinds of mistakes in what you've just typed. If you stop and scan your work for typos, don't correct everything you see; just change what the spell-checker won't. It's much quicker to choose **Change** in a spell check dialog box than it is to go back and fix every error.

Did you know that you can rename Program Manager? Control-drag any icon to copy it; it doesn't matter which icon, and to which place you drag it. Highlight the copy, go to **Properties** on the Program Manager File menu, select **Browse,** and go to your Windows directory. Choose **PROGMAN.EXE,** and select **OK** to go back to the Properties dialog box. You'll notice that the **Description** window says **Program Manager.** Alter this to anything you want–up to forty characters, spaces and punctuation allowed. Now select **OK** to return to Program Manager.

Other than your icon, you'll notice nothing else has changed. But, if you now double-click on the icon, Program Manager will have the name you chose. It will stay that way until you exit Windows. You can either double-click on the icon in subsequent sessions, or move the icon to the StartUp group to display your new name throughout the session. You may delete the icon without any problems.

This trick looks spectacular; unfortunately, it doesn't have many practical uses. It can be a memory jogger. You could call Program Manager "Grant Report due Tuesday!" or "Mary's Birthday Next Week." If you're Alt-Tabbing from application to application, a message such as this shows up when you expect to see Program Manager.

Of course, there are additional opportunities around the beginning of April. You could call Program Manager, "Windows 5.0 Beta 117h Confidential" or "Grateful Thanks—Bill G." This could also be accompanied by a story of your daring rescue of someone whose face you couldn't quite place, followed by his revelation that he owned Microsoft, and would give you anything for saving his life.

"So I told Bill, 'Just a personalized copy of Windows would be thanks enough.'"

Sadly, this trick doesn't work with any other program I've tried. It might be fun to work with "World's worst word processor," or "Most bug-ridden spreadsheet," but you can't change their names.

Program Features to Speed You Up

Most programs come with features to speed your work. If you're not using these, you're almost certainly working more slowly than you could be. Look to see if your program has any of the following:

- Styles
- Macros
- Scripts
- Master Pages
- Outliners
- Functions

Your programs may have some or all of these features, but may call them by different names.

Styles are collections of formatting instructions–you usually find them in word processing and page layout programs, and they are beginning to spread into other types of programs. When you've defined a style, you can apply the formatting to selected parts of your document or graphic with one mouse click.

You usually have to create styles by defining them and will discover that your program will guide you through the same dialog boxes you use to apply formatting changes one change at a time. Some programs let you select a style by example–place the cursor in a paragraph and all the formatting instructions are saved to apply to other paragraphs. Programs usually also come with some ready-made styles.

Use styles to apply formatting to similar parts of a document. For instance, this book has several types of headings and subheadings, and each one has a style. When I typed the book, these headings were typed as ordinary text. The style was applied later, by placing an insertion point in the paragraph then selecting a style.

Notice I've been referring to paragraphs when talking about styles. Most programs will only let you apply styles to entire paragraphs, although most programs treat a paragraph as any characters followed by a return. This means that you could type Section A <return> Overview of this report <return> The first steps <return>, and then apply different styles to each of the three paragraphs.

Styles have three advantages; speed, consistency, and flexibility. Once you establish a style it's easy to apply it time after time, page after page. Since you have styles for special parts of your document, Section Headings, for instance, will always be the same. Finally, you can change the definition of a style and all instances of it will change to reflect this. Suppose you format a hundred-page report and your boss decides that a particular type of subheading doesn't stand out enough. You may change them all individually, or change the style so that they all automatically change.

Macros appear mainly in word processors and spreadsheets, and are a set of instructions that you carry out so that the program can *learn* them. They can be run at any time by pressing a special key combination. Windows has a program–Recorder–which lets you create macros in any program. This is usually not as powerful as the macro capabilities of some programs.

At first glance macros may be mistaken for styles, but they are both more and less than styles. Styles restrict you to gathering formatting instructions, but macros let you use any program commands. However, macros merely automate commands, and once you've

195

used them to make changes the text (or spreadsheet) has no "memory" of how the change was made. In contrast, paragraphs with styles can be changed many times simply by redefining the style.

You may be reluctant to use macros. However, Microsoft is developing a whole language, called Basic for Applications. This will give you major power, but will only be available within Microsoft applications for Windows. However, expect the other companies to follow suit with macro languages of their own. There are already books written on WordBasic, the macro language which came with Word for Windows version 2.

These higher-level macros eventually read like lines of a program, and the obvious next step is to allow you to write scripts to carry out macro functions. There are scripts in PC Tools for Windows and Norton Desktop. PageMaker version 5 also has application-specific scripts.

Master pages are found most often in page layout programs, and let you place items such as a page number on a master page. These items will appear in the same position on every page. Page numbers from master pages automatically number correctly, and other master page items include headers and footers and graphic accents such as a line across the bottom of the text area.

Outliners are not like the other features mentioned here, but careful use of them will improve your writing. Outliners are found in word processors, and are the first step toward creating a long document.

Outlines consist of topics and subtopics, with several possible levels of sub-sub-topics. You create an outline by deciding which major topics you intend to cover. Then, break each topic down into subtopics. A general book on Windows might have two major topics; Windows itself and Windows applications. The section on Windows itself will probably break down into subtopics such as Program Manager, File Manager, and so on; these will probably be chapter titles. Similarly the section on Applications might contain subtopics such as word processors, spreadsheets, and so on; these too can be chapter titles.

Note that the two major points of an outline are shown in this example; the hierarchy, where topics break down into subtopics, and parallelism, where the section on Windows itself is mirrored in the section on applications.

As you develop an outline, you may find that a topic has many subtopics which appear to fall into two distinct groups. This is a sign that the topic should be split, and the outliner lets you do this. You may find that you have subtopics which fit better under another topic, and again the outliner lets you move them. The outliner will let you promote and demote subtopics.

If you develop an outline several levels deep, you may find that you've described the document completely. All that remains is to "fill in the blanks" which means that you have to write the text between the headings. You may want to use your topics and subtopics as headings, but you don't have to. Also, some words in your outline may not appear, such as try to think of other things to put here.

Outlines aren't for everyone, but if you must cover numerous points, they make it very easy for you to do this in a logical manner. They can even be used to write fiction, since all you have to do is organize the points of your plot.

Functions are like macros which have already been written for you. They appear in spreadsheets and are used to make common business calculations such as compound interest.

Cut and Paste and Search and Replace

You probably already know how to use these tools, but they can save you plenty of time if you use them to automate your work. If you cut and paste (or more often copy and paste), you can take a section of a document and reproduce it many times.

For instance, if you have to create a course catalog, you may need to list the title of the course, its reference number, the prerequisites, a description, the cost, hours, location, and dates the course is held. It makes sense to make one entry, copy and paste it as many times as necessary, and edit these entries rather than type the details and format from scratch. Until you cut or copy something else (or exit Windows), the details remain on the clipboard to be pasted as many times as necessary.

You can take this a step further. Suppose there are five locations, and these appear randomly over many entries. You could type them in full each time, or use the characters which appear over the five number keys. For instance, type !! to signify the first location, @@ to signify the second, and so on. When you've done this for every entry, search for !! and replace it with the full name of the first location. Using two exclamation marks avoids the possibility of changing exclamation marks that may appear in your text.

You might have to prepare a document which lists a month of dates in the format Wednesday, July 21, 1993. If you type , July , 1993 you can then copy and paste this into each place you need (notice the spaces and punctuation, that will appear in each entry.) Now, type a character from MTWHFSU as appropriate (to represent the days of the week) and also put the date in each entry. Finally, execute seven different search and replace operations to change the days to their full names.

198

OLE (Object Linking and Embedding)

You may have heard about this feature in Windows 3.1, but from what I've seen most people haven't tried it. With the advent of OLE version 2.0, (which is currently appearing in more and more applications), this technique will become crucial to working in Windows. I'll cover OLE version 2.0 in chapter ten; this section deals with OLE version 1.0.

You've already seen an example of OLE in chapter five, in the section on Object Packager. As you may recall, this feature lets you embed icons in documents, and these icons will open a file when double-clicked. In order for this to work, the icon files are attached to the main document file. So long as you have all the applications on another computer, you can save the document with embedded files to a diskette and give it to someone else to run on this machine.

However, there's a simpler use of OLE. If you create a graphic in Windows Paintbrush, you can embed it in another document. Here's how:

1. Create your drawing in Paintbrush (for demo purposes, any squiggle will do).

2. Select the tool which shows scissors and a rectangle (at the top of the right-hand column).

3. Position the cursor above and to the left of your drawing.

4. Drag the mouse to the bottom and right. As you do this, a dotted box appears around your drawing. When this box encloses the drawing, release the mouse.

5. Go to the Edit menu and select **Cut**. Go to the File menu and choose **Exit**. Say **No** to **Save Changes**. Your drawing is now on the **Clipboard**.

6. Open your word processor or Windows Write. Make certain the cursor is flashing.

7. Go to the Edit menu, and choose **Paste Special**. The Paste Special dialog box opens, with **Paintbrush Picture Object** highlighted. Click on the **Paste** button, and your drawing appears in the word processor.

Until now, this is just how any cut-and-paste operation would occur. However, let's suppose that you need to edit the drawing. If you had used a basic cut-and-paste, you'd have to select the drawing and cut it, close your word processor (unless you knew about Alt-Tab), open Paintbrush and paste the drawing back into it.

In Paintbrush you could edit the drawing, and then use the cut and paste method to place the drawing back in the word processor. Many people save the Paintbrush image so that it's easy to access, and so that the file appears once in the Paintbrush file directory and again as part of the document.

With OLE, much of this process is avoided. This is the way you edit:

1. Double-click on the drawing. Paintbrush opens with the drawing.

2. Edit as necessary, then go to the File menu.

3. There's a new command at the bottom of the menu: **Exit and return to [filename]**. The filename is the name of the file in the word processor.

4. Select this command and you return to the word processor with the edited version of your drawing in the same spot.

You can embed anything from any OLE-aware program into any other. Most programs are OLE-aware. Do you need a spreadsheet? Just embed that Excel spreadsheet into Ami Pro. Want a fancy table or equation in PageMaker? Make it WordPerfect for Windows and paste it in. Editing anything is a snap.

Now that you've reached this point in the book, you've probably realized that Windows is far more versatile than you ever suspected. But you may go further with just a little outside help in the form of an add-on program to extend Windows. These programs add a host of functions to Windows. So many in fact, that it can become confusing. However, in hunting for productivity, you will discover what's really useful and what's not.

Beyond Windows: Working with Desktop Shells

Although Windows has many strengths which aren't utilized by the average user, there comes a point when you begin to appreciate that there are some things you can't do, at least not with the Windows tools as they currently exist.

It almost seems as if programs, designed to extend Window's reach, are being released weekly. This section deals with just one—PC Tools for Windows—although almost every feature appears in one or more other programs. Norton Desktop for Windows has many similarities with PC Tools, but at the time of writing PC Tools was slightly more comprehensive.

If you are considering buying a program to improve Windows—and I think you should—then look carefully at the latest versions of these two programs, and any other programs that appear to cover the same territory. Take a good look even if you're not in the mood to buy, because these programs have features that will almost certainly turn up in the next version of Windows.

PC Tools for Windows

PC Tools, like Norton Desktop, came from the utility program market. These programs, often called the Swiss Army Knives of programs, were so named because they collected together a group of largely unrelated programs which carried out a variety of functions.

Data Recovery Programs. Although these programs now appear in DOS, utility programs tend to do thing a little better. You can undelete and unformat.

Disk Defragmentizers. These programs reorganize your disk so that each file fits into one area of the disk, not two or more. This speeds up disk reads, but can't be used with some versions of disk compression programs.

Backup Programs. You can use these to organize saving your data onto floppy disks or tape.

Antivirus Programs. Just like the newer versions of DOS, these programs will check your disk for viruses.

Disk Checking Software. Sometimes an entire disk fails; this can sometimes be repaired by using this software.

The important part of PC Tools and other programs, so far as this book is concerned, is their ability to enhance the Windows desktop. In the case of PC Tools, the entire desktop is replaced.

The PC Tools Desktop

When you start Windows with PC Tools installed, you won't see Program Manager. What you will see is one of several Desktops, which replace Program Manager as in figure 11-1. Switching between Desktops is like switching between alternate versions of Program Manager.

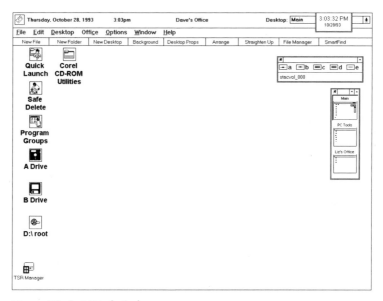

Figure 11-1. PC Tools Desktop

The default screen is called Joe's office, or whatever first name was used to register Windows (this was an embarrassment in my case, as I routinely register all software as belonging to Me, with a company called Us. So my office was called Me's Office).

The familiar line of icons across the bottom of your screen will be missing, replaced by one icon called program groups. Double-click on this icon and all your program group icons will appear inside a window. Because PC Tools can nest groups, they don't have to be spread out as before. Double-click on any program group icon and you'll see the same window that you saw before you installed PC Tools. You don't have to configure everything again.

On the right of your screen, you'll see the window displaying the other desktops. If you double-click on PC Tools, you'll open this desktop and see icons for many of the tools mentioned above. The third desktop is called Extra, and you can set this up to suit yourself. Also on the right is access to PC Tools' File Manager, and you double-click on a drive icon to see what's on a particular disk.

205

The remaining icons on the left of your screen allow you to print a file by dragging its icon onto the Print File icon, help you retrieve accidentally deleted files with SafeDelete, and launch programs and files instantly with Quick Launch.

Using PC Tools to Improve Productivity

Because PC Tools makes hundreds of changes to your Windows tools, there are many ways that you can improve productivity. Almost every aspect of the program can be customized, and you may spend a lot of time trying to see what's worthwhile.

The tool that I use most often—Quick Launch—has its own section later in the chapter, but there are many other tools which can help you get your work done quickly. The most improved part of PC Tools which has an immediate counterpart in Windows is the File Manager.

File Manager

If you configure File Manager in PC Tools you can have a row of icons across the top of the screen. This is called the **Toolbar,** and these icons control several features you won't find in Windows File Manager.

There is a command to show a window inside File Manager (PC Tools calls this a pane), which lets you view the contents of files created in any one of 50 formats. This is the **File Viewer,** and is useful when you can't identify a file from its name, or when you want to check whether you've selected the correct file before you delete it. You can search for text inside the File Viewer, and view compressed files before you decompress them.

You can compress and expand files in certain common compression formats, such as ZIP (version 1), .ARC, and .PAK. You may also scramble your files so they can be read only by using a password.

You can virus check one file, several, an entire directory, drive, or computer. If you have to delete a file containing sensitive material, you can overwrite it so the data can't be recovered.

I took some time to find one customizing feature that lets you position the Toolbar on any edge of the window, with text, pictures, or a combination of both.

Miscellaneous Tools

There are several other tools available in PC Tools which can speed your work. One that I use often is the SmartSearch tool, which not only finds files based on name, type, date created (and many variations of these); it also can find files based on content, and does this very quickly.

Content-based file searching usually means that you have to create an index of all the words used in the file, and the index file alone can be a large file which takes up space on your hard drive. PC Tools examines each file in turn to search for the text string, which is somewhat slower but usually more efficient. In order to make the search as short as possible, it's a good idea to carefully define the search criteria so that the fewest files are searched.

The program also has a defragmentizer, called Optimizer. This should not be used on many versions of compression software, such as Stacker—consult your documentation for details—but I use it regularly to make reports on the state of my compressed drives. You'll learn exactly what proportion of files are fragmented, and can even see which ones these are. If the drives need defragmentizing then I go to Stacker and use the SDEFRAG utility.

Scheduler is another useful tool which will display a message, launch a PC Tools utility, start a program, or start a program and open a file at the time you choose. You can do this once only, or have the action take place at intervals varying from a number of minutes to once a year. For example, you can also schedule events for every weekday, or the third Wednesday of the month. Unfortunately, Scheduler can't switch the computer on, so it has to be running to carry out any of these tasks.

If you have the slightest interest in programming, PC Tools has a scripting feature where you can write programs to carry out many actions within the program.

Quick Launch

I've talked about many ways of getting to your files in this book, but the Quick Launch feature of PC Tools comes closest to my ideal. Although this requires a little setting up, it provides you instant access to any file while you're running any program—this without searching through windows full of icons, and every document a click away.

I find this very useful when I'm working on a project and someone calls me with a query on some earlier work. I can reference all files relating to my caller and have a long file name to work with, instead of quitting the program and hunting through directories.

Configuring Quick Launch

PC Tools comes with a Quick Launch window; as configured, it doesn't look very worthwhile, with only four of the Windows accessories inside. When you press the CPS button at the extreme top left of any screen in any application, an enhanced Control Menu drops down. At the bottom of this is the Quick Launch command, which lists these four applications. If you select one, the program opens.

However, with a combination of renamed file icons you can put Quick Launch on steroids so that everything is close at hand. Here's how:

1. Open the **Quick Launch** window.

2. Open **PC Tools File Manager.**

3. **Drag** the icon for the file you need into the **Quick Launch** window.

4. Click on the name of the icon. A window opens in its place.

5. Type up to a 40 character file description.

6. Close the **Quick Launch** window. Your file now shows up on the **Quick Launch** list.

That's all you need to do. Some people prefer to put the file icon on the PC Tools desktop: This means you will soon fill the desktop with icons. Repeat the process outlined in the list above for every file you want to show in the Quick Launch list.

Configuring Quick Launch with Multiple File Windows

If you simply add file icons to the Quick Launch window, you'll end up with a longer and longer list—not conducive to easy searching. However, PC Tools has an ability that Norton Desktop doesn't (next version, maybe?)—it lets you nest windows inside the Quick Launch window.

I have put all my commonly used applications and files in Quick Launch. In order to keep the list manageable I've made sub-windows and sub-sub windows (PC Tools calls them folders). If you look at the arrangement of cascading menus in figures 11-2, you'll see that I'm pointing to the file called Letter to Brenda McLaughlin. Figure 11-3 shows the arrangement of windows to achieve this.

209

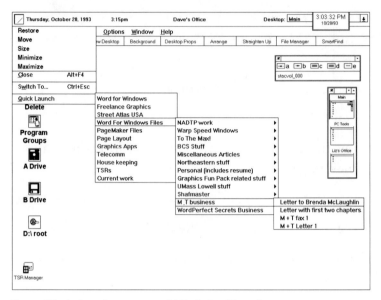

Figure 11-2. Cascading menus in PC Tools QuickLaunch

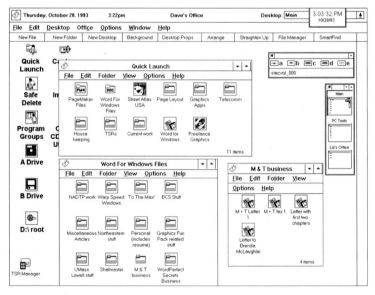

Figure 11-3. Arrangement of Windows to get Cascading Menus in Figure 11-2

By holding down control as you drag icons from other windows (not from File Manager) you can copy icons rather than moving them. This means that the same icon can turn up in different windows. Suppose you made estimates for several clients. You could store the file icon once in a window for the client, and again in a window called estimates.

You can quickly build a system by opening the Quick Launch Window and opening File Manager as soon as you quit a program. Drag the new file(s) into Quick Launch, create a long file description, and move everything into the relevant Window. This two-minute job keeps everything under control.

Now you can access any file at any time, because the CPS button stays on-screen at all times. It even appears in the corner of dialog boxes. Just one click and a longish drag will give you access to everything you've created. As you go through the folders, you'll get and idea of what the file refers to, so that when you come to the file name you'll be familiar with the type of information in the file.

The Quick Launch system gets around the major limitations of PC Tools; you cannot use Alt+Tab or Alt+Esc to change programs. You can use Control-Esc to bring up the task list, but you still cannot get to the Program Manager in PC Tools. However, you can put all the applications and files you normally look for onto the QuickLaunch list, so this isn't such a drawback.

Exploring PC Tools

I have spent a considerable amount of time experimenting with PC Tools, yet I feel that I've just scratched its powerful surface. Since the program can be customized in so many ways, I feel that the designers included this customization with the idea that the user would explore and use it.

If you build on what I have already presented here and experiment with the program, you may well come up with a novel way to achieve some productive effect. So don't accept the program at face value, explore and, who knows, what you may uncover!

In the next chapter, we'll look at that bane of Windows users—the system crash! Although these are far less frequent than they were in Windows 3.0, they can be confusing. Confusing in why they occur and how best to recover from them. I can't make crashes painless, but I can show you ways of avoiding the worst.

Crash and Burn

In a perfect world, we'd start our computers, run our applications, save our work, and always find the machine and our files ready and waiting for the next session. We'd spend our computing days without a care, knowing that we had 100 percent reliability.

Welcome to the real world.

You may be as productive as possible, and use every trick in this book, but if you are hit by crashes causing you to redo your work, then all of this is for nothing.

Hardware is not completely reliable, but it's getting better. What really throws us are software errors—right out of the blue, you'll get a message such as "APPLIC.EXE caused a General Protection Failure in OTHERAPP.EXE at A6603:5B7" (for the Windows programmers among you, I made the address up).

What happened? What did you do wrong? Can it be stopped? There's a lot involved in crash prevention, and much of it is in preparation. You can also recover from a crash with minimum damage. Let's try to make your computer as crash-proof as possible. You will never avoid crashes, but you can make them less likely.

Making Your Machine as Stable as Possible

Hardware and software crash damage can be minimized by not running the machine in a dangerous condition, thus preventing outside events from causing crashes, while being able to recover data with minimum loss. Here are some ways to configure your computer to run smoothly.

More RAM

If your machine tends to software crashes, it may be that two programs are trying to use the same area of RAM. "Two programs" doesn't have to mean two applications, such as a word processor and a spreadsheet; it may mean an application and Windows, or an application and a utility, such as Adobe Type Manager.

Windows manages RAM so that all programs receive a protected share; the more RAM, the easier it is for Windows to allocate sufficient memory. This should be handled by the RAM requirements of your programs. Almost all Windows programs run in four Megabytes, but some require more. If you have less than four megabytes, you may find that Windows works fine for most of the time, but will occasionally fail.

Check the memory requirements of all your programs. Remember that other programs such as SmartDrive may take up RAM space and cramp applications. Caches like SmartDrive do not require massive amounts of RAM to function efficiently; with four megabytes of RAM, you will need no more than half a Megabyte for your cache.

Don't simply add RAM as a cure-all, often the fault is a corrupted file (See the section on General Protection faults). Just be aware that a shortage of RAM can make crashes more likely.

UPS and Other Power Line Protection

Power failures are the number one source of Windows crashes—both at the time and later, when the program has to deal with corrupted files. Brownouts are possible at any time, and a tiny glitch will cause your computer to reset. Although power surges are more likely to damage your computer physically, power failures are most likely to cause you to lose data.

No computer should be operated without a some kind of surge protection. There are different degrees of protection, but for many of us the most cost-effective method is a $10 power strip..It will cost more than $100 to achieve significantly better surge protection .

Power surges come from two places; the outside of your building, from lightning strikes and power supply fluctuations, and inside the building, when heavy machinery is switched on. The low-cost power strip will deal with almost all of these, but if your computer is running mission-critical work, you should look into more expensive protection. You'll probably need a professional electrician to determine the actual causes.

The best solution is a UPS (Uninterruptible Power Supply). This is a box containing a battery and circuitry to ensure that when the power supply is disrupted, the battery supplies you with power for a few minutes; long enough to exit your applications gracefully and not lose any data.

A UPS costs under $200. Follow the manufacturer's instructions about which size to purchase for your computer. A small UPS may be cheap, but if it cannot supply sufficient power, it may cause the computer to crash when the power cuts out. For my 486-66, with 17 inch monitor and CD drive, I use a 400 VA UPS.

Don't connect peripherals to the UPS, unless you've bought one large enough to support them. If you're printing and you lose power, it's easy enough to start the print run from the point where you stopped. Therefore, there's no need to connect the printer to the UPS.

Your monitor should be connected to the UPS. You obviously can't exit programs easily without a monitor, but if your monitor suddenly dies, try the following:

1. Press **Alt-F4**. (This is the same as choosing Exit).

2. Press **Enter**. (This chooses Save Changes).

3. Type a file name, unless your document has previously been saved. Even if it has been saved, typing a file name will not affect the process.

4. Press **Enter** if you're saving the file. This saves the file and exits the program. Again, this won't affect the process if the file is already saved.

5. Press **Alt-F4**. (This is the same as choosing Exit Windows).

6. Press **Enter**. This confirms that you want to exit Windows.

7. Wait about ten seconds to be sure that your computer has returned to DOS, and then switch it off.

216

If you lose power and have a UPS connected, you'll hear series of beeps. When power fluctuations occur, you may also hear a beep now and then. If the power goes out completely, it's obvious that you must exit Windows. If the power is just fluctuating, switch on a lamp to check that the power is still there.

Tape Backup

There are many different forms of backup, and many strategies associated with them. Almost all of them fail because we see them as too much trouble. However, that's nothing compared with the time needed to restore lost data.

The best form of backup is the easiest, and a tape drive is probably that. A 250 Megabyte tape drive costs under $200, and tapes around $25. These drives are made by Colorado, Iomega, and other brands, and are also available as "own-brands" by other suppliers.

Tape backup is slow, but this may be an advantage. There's always something to do other than work on the computer, and this can be scheduled for the last part of the day, while the tape is backing up. The first backup is the longest since the entire drive has to be saved. At a top speed of 4-5 Megabytes a minute, this can take a long time.

After the first, you need only make incremental backups, which saves the data created since the last save. This can often take just a few minutes, so it's ideal for "no-brainer" backups at the end of the day. Since tapes need to be formatted, which takes over an hour, you may want to buy pre-formatted tapes.

Expansion Card Overload

One great advantage of PCs is their ability to take many expansion cards. Unlike some other computers, a PC's power supply is large enough to handle several cards without problems, but software control of cards is fraught with problems.

You often have to configure cards by moving jumpers (small connecting pieces), and set the software to suit. As you add cards, this process becomes more complicated, because any card may have incompatibilities with any other.

Most people manage to set up expansion cards with no trouble, but some have continuing problems which often lead to machine instability and crashes. A few cards refuse to co-exist, no matter how you try. You may have to call the manufacturers to sort out your problems. This may be a thing of the past with Intel's Plug 'n' Play standard which enables boards to run without clashing and lets you set them up in software, without having to reset jumpers.

Don't run with the cover off

Some components in your computer run hot, particularly the CPU. If run over its designed temperature, you may give spurious errors. Computer designers are well aware of this, and put one or more fans inside the case to keep the temperature down.

These fans receive a predictable airflow to do their job, and if you run your computer with the cover off you'll change the flow of air. This means that the CPU can get dangerously hot, as well as the possibility of dust being pulled into diskette and CD drives.

So keep the cover on your machine to ensure the safest results.

Disk compression—a danger?

There are several disk compression schemes such as DOS's own DoubleSpace and programs like Stacker. I use Stacker and have never had problems, but some people have removed disk compression software due to crashes.

In cases like this it's impossible to know exactly what was causing the problem, and it's very easy to blame the compression software when something else may have been at fault. I intend to go on using disk compression, and the new drive that I've just bought will have disk compression on it from day one.

Planning to avert disaster

Since it's impossible to be certain you won't get hardware or software crashes, you should try to work in a manner that places you at least risk.

Using Timed Backups and Other File Strategies

Many programs now have a timed backup feature. This is a very important resource to save yourself from crashes. Make certain that yours is always on, and set to save as often as possible.

This feature doesn't usually save like a regular Save or Save as command. I'm typing this book in Word for Windows, which has created a hidden file with the same name as my file name, except that the first two characters are ~$ and the last two are discarded. So if you created a file called RALPHLET.DOC, there would be a backup file called ~$RALPHL.DOC, created by the timed backup.

Since Word for Windows appends changes to the end of the file when you make a fast save (like many other applications), the timed backup feature just adds these to the backup file. When you Save, the program appends these and deletes the backup file. If you Save As, the program puts all changes in their correct place. Finally, when you exit the program and say Save Changes, all appended changes are also placed correctly.

If you have a system crash, when you next start Word, it automatically displays all files that were open at the time of the crash with the word (Recovered) displayed after the file name. You should be able to find the file that lets you start work again with a minimum of data loss.

This method works well, with one exception. If you haven't named the file you can't be sure what it's called. Word tries to use the date and time, but you'll make your life much easier if you get into the habit of naming files as soon as you've started the document. This is good practice for any program. If you regularly use the keyboard shortcut for Save, you'll protect yourself.

Virus Checking

So much had been written about viruses, that it's natural to assume any unexplained happening means you have one. The actual proven occurrences of viruses falls far short of the number of times they have been used as an explanation. Very few virus writers have small enough egos to create a virus that does its work in secret; they prefer to display a message on your screen to tell you that it's their virus that's trashing your hard drive.

However, viruses are out there, and they can lead to you having to recreate your work just like a system crash. You will almost certainly receive any virus you encounter from a floppy disk. If the floppy comes from a computer which handles many people's disks, it's very likely that viruses may be around. I find about one virus-infected disk about every eighteen months—the last two came from a college computer lab and a music store.

You're very unlikely to get a virus from a shareware disk or bulletin board. Both types of organizations rigorously check files through the best virus scans to make certain that no viruses exist. Bulletin boards have sections for new uploaded files that aren't available to the public until the sysop (system operator) has given them a going-over.

Obviously, you need an anti-virus program which will detect viruses automatically. There are a number of these around, including the version in DOS 6. If you use other people's floppy disks in your computer, you owe it to yourself to get one and use it.

One way to help a virus get in your system is to leave a floppy disk in the drive when you boot up. This is when your computer is most at risk. Get into the habit of taking floppies out of the drive before you start the computer.

Save at Appropriate Times

There are certain times when you are more at risk from a system crash. Some operations are more complex than others. It's always a good idea to save before you print, spell check, search and replace, or cut and paste.

Disk Recovery Systems

DOS now has some of the tools that the utility programs have for recovering files. These tools are not so much an aid to recovering damaged files as a way of saving you from your errors, with tools such as Undelete and Unformat.

Modern IDE hard disks take care of errors that used to show up in earlier formats. The electronics on the disk automatically detect bad sectors and make certain the operating system can't write data to them.

General Protection Faults

The most common error message in Windows is the General Protection Fault, or GPF. You'll see a message that says one program caused a fault in another. Make a note of the file names so that you can repair the damage.

What the Messages Mean

When you get a GPF message the computer is telling you that two programs can't co-exist. This is usually due to a corrupted file in one program. As Windows programs consist of many files, use the

Search command on File Manager's File menu to find any files that you can't identify. Their location will give you a clue as to which program uses them. For instance, if the file is in the FLW directory, it's part of the Freelance Graphics for Windows group of files.

Some programs affect several different programs. I once had a system crash that corrupted Adobe Type Manager. Each time I tried to print from any program, there was a GPF that mentioned ATM.EXE. It was obvious that the fault lay with this file.

It's not always obvious which of the two files mentioned is at fault. The simplest method is to assume both need attention. If you're a skilled programmer, you may be able to tell exactly what's going on, but most of will have to use the brute force method–reinstalling.

What You Should Do

When it's likely that a file's corrupted, you'll have to reinstall one or both of the suspect programs. This may sound like a major undertaking, but it often passes painlessly. It's unlikely that you'll lose any configuration settings, since most Windows applications save these as a file. When the program installs or reinstalls, it looks to see if this file is present. If it's not, the file is created. If it is, the rest of the program is installed around it.

Often, the installation program looks first to see if the application directory exists. This saves having to examine all disks and partitions to see if there's sufficient space for all the files, and to have to create the directory itself. You may get a dialog box that asks if you want to overwrite the current program files; obviously, choose yes.

One thing you will not lose is your data files. Program installation routines will only overwrite, not delete. If you reinstall into a new directory, you'll have to manually move the files across to the new directory using File Manager, but that's the only problem.

Incompatibility

Very rarely, you may find that even after you reinstall both programs you may still experience the same GPFs. This could be because the programs are incompatible–that is, due to bad design, they can't coexist on the same machine.

This is the time to check the README files that came with each program–chances are that someone's already picked up this fault and has devised a work-around. There may be a way to get what you want by running one program in a slightly different way.

If you still can't find the problem you'll have to call tech support for each company. If you have one of those agreements where you get ninety days' support from the first call, or you're already out of the free tech support period, call anyway. Explain that there appears to be an inconsistency between the two programs, and you don't see why you should have to pay for support if the two programs will not run together. The companies should be as concerned as you are to eliminate these problems.

It may be that there's no way around the incompatibilities. I have one game program that causes a crash in KRNL386.EXE in the Windows System directory. This file is the Kernel of Windows— hence the name—yet the game company insists that it's my video driver that's at fault. Hmm. In the meantime, I don't run the game.

Dr. Watson

If you know the Sherlock Holmes stories, you'll know that Doctor Watson was the fictional scribe who recorded all of Holmes's doings. That's what the Dr. Watson program does with Windows.

If everything is working fine, Dr. Watson does nothing. However, you have a crash, the program springs into action and records the contents of many of the internal registers of the CPU. Don't expect to understand it; unless you're a Windows programmer, you won't.

223

But to a company trying to track down an obscure fault, Dr. Watson is a lifesaver.

If you can't find the icon, use the methods described earlier in the book to drag it out of the Windows directory in File Manager. The file is called DRWATSON.EXE, and you can put in the StartUp group window; you don't even have to check the run minimized box, because the program naturally runs this way.

Until you have a crash, you'll see a dialog box that tells you "No faults detected," and you can click the OK button to return to your application. If there is a GPF or similar fault, the program has a long file, which you can print or save to floppy disk, and send to the manufacturer. Maybe I'll use it on that game the manufacturers say is crashed by my video driver. That should point the finger.

BOOTLOG.TXT

If Windows crashes as your session starts, you can see what the problem is in a file called BOOTLOG.TXT. This is in your Windows directory, and you can look at it in a DOS word processor or line editor. It's just a list of processes attempted, with enigmatic explanations such as LoadStart and LoadSuccess, and INIT and INITDONE.

It's probably not the most gripping thing you'll ever read, but to a tech support person it can save hours of guesswork. You can double-click on the icon in File Manager, and see the contents in Notepad.

Recovering from a crash

The worst has happened; you've had a crash and are back in DOS. Is everything lost? Not necessarily. Some programs come with parachutes; your files may turn up almost undamaged.

Checking the TEMP Directory

The place to look for the missing files is in your TEMP directory. Look at your AUTOEXEC.BAT file; it may have a line that says SET TEMP=C:\TEMP. If you have a line like this, it's obvious where your TEMP directory is. Sometimes you'll see a line such as SET TEMP=C:\DOS. This means that all your temporary files will be stored in the DOS directory. I prefer to create a TEMP directory and then insert the appropriate line in the AUTOEXEC.BAT, rather than hunting around the DOS directory.

As programs carry out certain processes, they may store a version of the file in the TEMP directory. If there's a crash, these files remain. If the program finishes normally, the files are deleted. The files are easy to spot; they end in .TMP or the file name starts with the tilde character (~). The files may be useless; some have a size of zero bytes, which doesn't hold out much hope for recovery. However, some may be the right size (similar to the file you were working on), and with some judicious renaming, you can open them in the program which created them.

Some programs have unusual ways of saving files. PageMaker stores a copy of the file in the TEMP directory every time you turn to a new page or perform other functions. You can end up after a crash with several files, all of which could be the one you need. If you use File Manager's View menu, and sort by date, the most recent file will be first. Rename this and open it in PageMaker. If it's not what you'd hoped for, try the next earlier file until you find a file in a workable condition.

Missing files can turn up in other places as well. They can sometimes be found in the root directory of your C: drive, or in the place where the rest of the files of this program would be stored.

Windows has moved from being a poor imitation of the Mac, to a workable alternative, and soon to something that will have a character of its own. Great changes are just around the corner, and may even be here by the time you read this. Just as you've seen how apparently superfluous features of Windows can have major effects on productivity, so the new operating systems on the way will have many powerful tools to speed your work–if you know how to use them. In the next chapter, we'll look at what's in store and how to take advantage of it.

13

Warp Speed to the Future

Everything you know about computers is wrong.

Well, maybe not everything, but this is as good a place as any to start looking at what's going to happen to mainstream computing in the next few years.

You may have thought that you'll be running a Microsoft operating system on an Intel-chip computer for the foreseeable future. You might, you might not. The categories we've used to define computers are breaking down, and there will be a period of retrenchment while the smoke clears.

This may sound like a problem, but it's all to the good. No company can afford to bring out overpriced products; no company can afford to produce half-baked products. Computer buyers are savvy enough not to choose dead-end systems, and they are smart enough not to need hand-holding from the manufacturers.

The market is king, and it decides which products survive, and which won't. We first saw this several years ago, when IBM introduced their PS/2 computers with the Micro Channel Architecture (MCA) bus. This product, more revolutionary in its day than local bus, was supposed to be the new standard. IBM expected to collect a hefty royalty from licensing its use to other companies.

This never happened. Nowadays IBM sells PS/2 computers to its corporate customers, but the computers for the rest of us–the PS/1s, the ValuePoint series–conform to the market standard. IBM thought they were going to take computing in a new direction, but when they looked around, the rest of the players were still carrying on as before. MCA has become a liability, rather than an asset. If you own one of these computers, you have to buy special expansion boards, because the normal ones won't fit.

These market forces shape the way in which all computer products are designed and sold. Operating systems such as Windows are subject to the same pressures.

What We Want From an Operating System

There are many qualities required of an operating system. Some are complementary to each other, some are exclusive. If operating systems cost $500, or ran in 32 Megabytes of RAM, they'd be a lot different than these available today. But no one would pay that much, or install that amount of RAM. There are some definite rules.

It must be backward compatible. There are over 30 million Windows users, each with an average of five applications. There are approximately another 70 million DOS users, who will eventually upgrade. Therefore, any operating system must let these users run their applications.

It must be relatively cheap. When you can change versions of DOS for under $50, then an upgrade cannot cost more than $100. In Windows there is as much code as a full-fledged application, and the testing for compatibility is endless. Although the cost is low, the volume is great, so the profit works out be about the same, if not more.

It must have reasonable machine requirements. When Windows 3.0 came out, four megabytes of RAM was a rarity, and hard drives of 40 Megabytes were considered large. Now four Megabytes of RAM is standard, with many computers being sold with eight or 16 Megabytes. Similarly, a typical machine now has a 200 Megabyte hard drive.

It must be easy to use. This is a form of backwards compatibility. We don't want operating systems that require us to radically rethink how we work. Windows required that from DOS users, which probably accounts for the large number of them who haven't made the change. Windows NT is very similar to Windows itself–the interface is almost exactly alike.

Operating systems that appear must fill these conditions.

The Future of Windows

Microsoft is committed to Windows and its variants as the operating system of today and tomorrow. From the news already been released about the next generation of Windows, it is clear that they will make radical rather than gradual changes. As Windows 3.0 transferred Windows from a curiosity into a workable system that people actually wanted to use, so new versions of Windows will change in a revolutionary way.

While it's possible to guess about Windows 4.0, one product that's already been released. Windows NT, gives some clues as to where Windows is heading.

Windows NT

Windows NT is the most advanced operating system Microsoft has ever released, and it stands comparison with anything that's out there. It has the following advantages over Windows 3.1.

It's not DOS-based. This means that all the problems associated with DOS, like eight character file names, can be forgotten.

It has built-in networking. This is industrial-strength standard, not a simple and slow method found in some other systems. Network security is built-in at the operating system level, which means much more protection.

It's a 32-bit system. This means that it runs faster than an equivalent 16-bit system, like Windows 3.1.

It has built in multi-tasking. Windows 3.1 multi-tasking is a form of time-sharing of the CPU; if one application crashes, you have to stop all of them and start again. Windows NT keeps applications separate, so if one crashes, the others will continue to run.

It has built-in multi-threading. Programs may be written with multiple threads—in other words, processes can run in parallel. This, of course, makes no difference without the next feature . . .

It supports multiple processors. Computer not fast enough? Add another processor. Depending on the program, you'll see major performance gains. Even if your programs don't lend themselves to multi-threading, you'll gain with multi-tasking using multiple processors.

Runs on different processors. You won't need an Intel chip to run NT. It can work with other processors that are not Intel-compatible.

The downside of Windows NT, and the reason why we haven't all rushed out and bought it, is that it costs several hundred dollars, requires 12 Megabytes of RAM, and around seventy Megabytes of disk space. NT runs DOS and Windows in emulation, so that software makes these applications "see" the system as a normal DOS machine. You need Windows NT-specific applications to take the most advantage of it.

If you could take the best parts of Windows 3.1 and Windows NT and combine them into an operating system that fit the way you worked, perhaps you'd say:

"I like the power of NT, but I don't need the networking power, at least not as strong as that which NT provides. Nor do I care if it runs on non-Intel processors. But I love the idea of long file names, faster processing, multi-tasking and multi-threading; can't the RAM and disk space requirements be lower?"

Welcome to Windows 4.0.

Windows 4.0

By the end of 1994, Windows 4.0 will be the new operating system. This is not an upgraded Windows 3.1, but rather, an altered Windows NT. DOS 7 will be released, but this will not be required to run Windows 4.0, because Windows will no longer run under DOS.

You'll buy one product that will replace both DOS and Windows. Windows 4.0 will be much closer to Windows NT in structure, even though at first glance, it will look like Windows 3.1. There are several factors which will shape the way it looks:

The Windows NT basis. This includes almost all the features described above.

The features from utility programs. DOS has gradually added features from utility programs. Some of the features from Norton Desktop and PC Tools for Windows will appear in Windows 4.0.

The Apple connection. With the virtual end of Apple's suit against Microsoft, which charged copying of Mac operating system features in Windows, expect several of the features in the Mac's operating system to appear.

The Warp Speed features. No, Microsoft didn't ask me what to put in the new version, but in the three years since Windows began, Microsoft has obviously been watching what people do with the program and planning improvements.

I expect to see the following features:

File Manager and Program Manager in one. This has already been leaked to the press. It could be like the Norton and PC Tools approach, with disk icons on the desktop, or it could be something entirely new.

Nested windows. If PC Tools and Norton can do this, Windows 4.0 can.

Some form of better networking. Maybe the inclusion of Windows for Workgroups. If not, strong links to a (Microsoft-specific?) network program.

The ability to run DOS, Windows 3.1, and Windows NT applications. This is key to the Microsoft strategy, and will mean that software companies can drop their Windows 3.1 versions of applications and move straight to NT (see later in this chapter what happens to those who stay with Windows 3.1).

A familiar interface. Don't look for anything wild. The program will be radically different from Windows 3.1, but the interface will be reassuringly similar.

The built-in utilities you've come to expect in DOS. What's special about these? Remember, the program isn't based on DOS. All the utilities you use which are DOS-based (like compression programs, disk defragmentizers, and so on) *will not run* under Windows 4.0. But they'll be a part of it.

One major part of Windows 4.0 will be OLE 2.0. I will discuss this later in the chapter, but don't assume that this is some arcane feature of Windows you'll never use. OLE 2.0 will change the way you work forever, and will probably be one of the most talked-about features of the program (although it's already available in Windows 3.1).

Win 32s

I don't know what the RAM and hard drive requirements will be for Windows 4.0, but I suspect that they will be greater than Windows 3.1. If you don't have the power to run 4.0, will you miss out on NT applications?

No. Microsoft has at present another product, called WIN32s. This is an addition to Windows 3.1, and will let you run NT applications on your present computer. You won't get many of the benefits that come with NT or Windows 4.0, but at least you won't have to buy a Windows 3.1 application now and upgrade it when you can afford to move to a more advanced version of Windows.

This means that no matter what your plans—stay with Windows 3.1, move to Windows 4.0, or change to Windows NT–NT applications will work with all three of these. As you upgrade, you'll unleash more of the power in the application.

There won't be a "chicken-and-egg" situation, where people won't move to a new operating system because there are not enough applications, and software companies won't develop applications for the new system because not enough people are using it. Instead, the market for NT applications will grow considerably within a few months, because many people will have the means to run them.

Windows at Work

As if all of this wasn't enough, Microsoft has realized that many pieces of office machinery are just specialized computers, and has proposed an interface standard so that they may connect to your computer.

This interface, called Windows at Work, will play a most important part in your selection of equipment. You could create a document in your word processor and run it off the copier without ever having it printed. The control panels of your office equipment will look more like a Windows screen.

Windows alternatives

There are a few operating systems being created by companies other than Microsoft which provide many of the features of Windows. The NeXT company, which used to make the NeXT computer, now sells their NeXTStep operating system for Intel-chip computers. Some of the companies that have UNIX-based software plan to release it for Pentium-based computers.

Rumors continue that Apple plans to release its system software to run on Intel-chip machines, though the applications you may buy will have to be those for the Macintosh.

All of these operating systems suffer from a dearth of applications compared to Windows, and even though the Macintosh has the largest selection, almost anything on Macintosh is already available for Windows.

The Future of Hardware

Microsoft's intention to release Windows NT for non-Intel chip computers has caused a flurry of activity by manufacturers such as Digital and MIPS. New machines from the Apple-IBM partnership may be included in the NT stable. Naturally, as the largest CPU maker in the world, Intel is not standing idly by.

234

Non-Intel machines

If a manufacturer builds a computer which runs Windows NT, it provides that machine with the ability to run the largest selection of software in the world. This has not been lost on several manufacturers who have hitherto addressed the workstation market.

Since the Pentium chip provides power enough to equal most workstations, the workstation market will be absorbed into the general desktop computer market. However, the workstation makers won't have to buy Intel CPUs as all the clone makers do, and then have to compete on price. Instead, they can use their own chips and compete on power.

Digital has brought out the Alpha computer, which they say will run twice as fast as Pentium-equipped computers. Other manufacturers are also bringing out their own machines.

Power PC

You may have read some time ago that both IBM and Apple decided to join together to produce a computer which would be manufactured by both companies. IBM linked with Motorola (the suppliers of CPUs for Apple machines) and they have now produced the Power PC chip, which will go into IBM machines, new Apple machines, and will also be available for clone manufacturers.

The Power PC chip is about as powerful as the 66 MHz Pentium on normal calculations, but faster on floating-point math. This is a characteristic of RISC (Reduced Instruction Set Computing) machines.

IBM and Apple have combined to create an operating system for the Power PC called Taligent, but this is not expected for some time. By the time this book is published, Microsoft may have announced that they will release Windows NT for Power PC. A recent survey indicated that over a third of potential Power PC buyers wanted to use it.

Intel chips

Where does all this leave Intel? They stated, when they launched the Pentium, that they don't expect to produce significant quantities until 1994, and that the 486 chip would be their major part output until then.

At one time, Intel gave out details of new chips long before they were available, but lately they have been keeping a low profile. This doesn't mean that they have nothing to announce, but rather that they have plans they wish to keep confidential.

When the Pentium was announced, long before it became available, Intel revealed that they were working on new chips with parallel sets of development teams. This hasn't received much press lately, but it was interesting to see a New York Times interview with the developer of the Pentium. He stated, now that the chip was released, he was working on the P7 chip, which the Times called the successor to the Pentium.

This might sound plausible enough except that the Pentium's codename was the P5. When the chip was announced, it was also revealed that parallel development teams were creating new CPUs to reduce the time to market. The successive generations of chips were called the P5, P6, and P7. What happened to the P6? Maybe it was a ploy by Intel to confuse their rivals, or maybe this chip will be launched some time in 1994.

In the meantime, the Pentium line will probably be upgraded, just like the 486. The 486 more than doubled in speed over its life, and the rumored "clock-tripler" 486-99 DX3 could extend its life even further. It's probable that there are clock-doubled Pentiums in the wings, and there has been talk of 100 MHz chips.

Another view I've seen is that Intel must make the break with the CPUs which run DOS. Intel has made their own RISC chips that can stand comparison with Power PC chips, but these cannot run

DOS. Currently, any new CPU that Intel releases must be backward compatible with every previous chip, right back to the 8088 which powered the first PC.

With Windows 4.0 not needing DOS, the stage is set for an operating system that resembled Windows 4.0 as to applications, but would work with a totally new chip design. This would mean that the entire chip design could change without users having to buy new applications.

OLE 2.0

OLE 1.0 is an unappreciated part of Windows. I covered this in detail in a previous chapter. Simply put, it allows you to create links between an object and its creating application, like an illustration that you embed into another document. Double-click on the illustration and you enter the creating application in order to edit it. Where the exit command used to be, the command is exit and return to the document.

This is a quick method for editing an embedded object. One of the less important features of OLE 2.0 is the ability to edit an embedded object without leaving the document in which it's embedded. Double-click on the object and the view of the document remains the same. However, if you look at the menus, you'll see that they now have the commands from the illustration program, and you'll also see any toolbars or other on-screen tools. Make your edit, and you can "return" to your document.

Automated OLE

If that was all that OLE 2.0 did, it would be a useful improvement over version 1.0. But the major change in OLE 2.0 is a process called automated OLE. What does this mean?

An application doesn't "own" a document any more.

Ever since you started computing, everything you produced was created by an application. You could open that application, and the document could be opened within it. "Document" could then mean a word processed file, a spreadsheet, a database—any file produced by an application.

You may have used more than one application to produce a document. You could make a drawing in an illustration program and use it in a word processed letter. You could take a spreadsheet and put it in a desktop published report. But ultimately one application "owned" that document.

Not any more.

With OLE 2.0, you may use more than one application, not just at different stages of the document's creation, but *at the same time, on the same screen.* Part of the document can be created in one program, part in another.

The ramifications of this go much deeper. It raises the question, What is an application? Why choose between applications, when you can have the best of both? Imagine choosing two complementary applications, each having the strengths the other lacks, and creating super-documents with them.

Desktop publishing programs such as PageMaker and Quark Xpress give you the ability to add small programs to enhance the original features. With OLE 2.0 every program has this ability. Imagine WordPerfect Helper, a program to seamlessly add certain features to WordPerfect for Windows. It doesn't exist yet, but it probably will.

OLE 2.0 is already available, but because it has only appeared gradually most people haven't noticed it. Software manufacturers are building it into their programs as versions change, but expect just about every program to have it by mid-1994.

You'll find that OLE 2.0 will affect the way in which you work more and more. It's such a powerful tool, you can't ignore it.

238

Windows 4.0 will build heavily on it, and if you take the time to understand it you'll find many new ways to speed up your work.

How To Run Any Computer at Warp Speed

Warp Speed Windows was written about Windows 3.1, but the truth is, it could be written about any computer or software, past, present or future. Until manufacturers take the time to point out the productivity features in their hardware and software, you'll have to use books like this or find out for yourself.

I approached all the features in Windows with one thing in mind–how can this help everyday computing? Just because Windows gives you the chance to change something, it doesn't mean that it has to be useful. When you look at other programs and even other computers, ask yourself these questions:

- Are the commonly-used ways of working necessarily the most productive?

- Is there some way of reconfiguring my equipment to improve productivity?

- Are there productivity features of which I'm not aware?

- Do other programs and computers do things in a better way?

I encourage you to look at other programs and computers to develop experience of how things can be done differently. Much of what I discovered in Windows was through an attempt to achieve some of the features you can find on the Apple Macintosh. In my opinion, although Windows 3.1 is not quite as good as the Macintosh System 7 software, it's interesting to see that in many cases there wasn't a better or a worse way to accomplish something–just a different way.

What appear to be drawbacks in Windows can be strengths. Since the icons in Program Manager don't represent anything but a pointer to programs, you may delete them without worrying. On the Mac, to delete icons mean that you'd deleted the program. Warp Speed Windows techniques can be applied to the Mac, where appropriate. For instance, you can create an "everyday" window on the Mac and use aliases to put all the icons in it that start programs, even if you have several drives.

Be aware of productivity; look for it in tip sections of magazines, and in reviews of programs. Be your own *Warp Speed* expert by focusing on productivity wherever you can find it.

It's Not the Computer, It's The Operator

If you've read this far, you'll probably have picked up a number of time-saving tips which will change the way you compute. But the real message of this book is not in any of the chapters or the Instant Gratification section–it's in the Introduction. Go back and re-read it. Try to arrange your work habits so that you can be more productive through faster typing, methodical working, and uninterrupted sessions at the computer.

Do this, follow the instructions in this book, and you'll truly work at Warp Speed.

Index

.BMP 94
.DOC 81
    file 114, 150
.EXE 126
    file 41, 44
.TMP 81
286 68, 76
386 68-69, 76, 90, 179
    Enhanced 52
386SPART.PAR 53
386SX 69, 92
486 69, 76-77, 179, 236
    chip 236
    computer 91
    machine 73
486-25 77
486-25SX 92
486-50DX2 78
486-66 77-78, 80, 92
    local bus board 90
486-99 DX3 236
486SX 69
    computer 90
486SX-25 77
80286 68 series see also 286
80386 68 series see also 386
80486 68 series see also 486

A

accelerated video card 77, 82, 85, 91
accelerators 71
accented characters 168
Accessories 119
    group 22, 24, 46, 54, 129
accessory 153
active window 103
Adobe

    format 112
    Type 1 fonts 86
    Type Manager 95, 112
aliases 240
Alpha computer 235
Alt key 57-58, 133, 149, 168
    combinations 169
Alt+Esc 175, 211
Alt+Tab 56, 58, 60-61, 123, 175-179, 184, 186-188, 200, 211
Always on Top 48
analog 95
Antivirus Programs 204
Appearance window 159
Apple 235
    Macintosh 95, 239
Apple-IBM partnership 234
applets 95, 100, 155, 160, 164-165, 167, 170
application 30, 48, 51, 58-59, 186, 214, 238
    file 126
    install 119
    linked 41
    start 40
    starts 37
    window 98, 122, 129
applications 13, 15, 21, 23, 30, 44, 87, 94, 191, 209, 213
    open 29
    Windows NT 232
archiving 138
Arrange Icons 120, 122
ASCII format 156
ASSOCIAT.DOC 30
Associate 44
    command 149, 151
    With Box 44
asterisks 166

AT bus 70
Auto Arrange 27, 122
AUTOEXEC.BAT 82, 148, 156, 161, 225
automate commands 195
automated OLE 237
Average access time 81

B
backup 138
    file 219
Backup Programs 204
basic machine 76
BOOTLOG.TXT 224
Brownouts 215
Browse 44, 126, 134, 193
    button 41
Bulletin boards 164, 220
buried commands 96
business
    applications 77
    computer 75
    computing 171
    machines 76

C
cache 71-73, 79, 84
    Hard drive 73
    hit 72
    memory 78
    miss 72
    RAM 72
    SmartDrive RAM 72
Cache Memory 67
    speeds 71
Caches 215
caching hard drive controllers 77
calculations 167
calculator 54, 56, 166, 185
    scientific 167
    tape 167
Calendar 164-165
Cardfile 164-165
Cascade 16, 123-125
CD drive 216
Change 193
    button 52
    Icon 36, 41, 133
Character
    Man 185
    Map 54, 56, 59, 127, 167, 169-170, 187
Characters to Copy 169
checkmark 106
Circuit board 80
    design 67

clip board 166
Clock 47-48, 54, 56, 95, 110, 153, 161, 167, 179, 185
    icon 46
    speed 68, 77
    window 49, 154
Close button 187
codes 170
color 83, 108
    schemes 108
command 107
    Associate 149, 151
    buried 96
    Delete 148
    Quick Launch 208
    Save 106, 219
    Save As 219
    Search 222
    Sets Fonts 154
Command Line 39, 134, 148
    box 152
commands 106, 190
    automate 195
    key 169
    keyboard 162, 168
common compression formats 206
communications program 163
Compaq 66
complex
    Database 74
    programs 74
    spreadsheet 74
component manufacturers 66
Compressed drives 86
compression programs 232
CompuServe 85
computer
    assemblers 66, 73
    instructions 5
    power 8
computer-based skill 76
configuration 222
configure cards 218
configuring Windows 189
Content window 158-159
context-sensitive help 107
Control 38
    key 23, 146
    menu 47-48, 208
    Panel 50-51, 53, 108, 153, 175, 177
Control-drag 128, 148
Control-dragging 185
Control-Shift-I 192
CONTROL.EXE 177

242

Cool Switch 55-56, 176
coprocessor 78, 90
copy 60, 198
    button 169
    icons 54, 128
    Package 159
    to Windows 112
correct
    description 146
    icon 146
    path 146
corrupted file 221
CPS button 208, 211
CPU 6, 68-69, 72-73, 83, 92, 223, 230, 237
    cache 78
    chip 67, 77
    manufacturers 73
    power 6
    speed 78
crash 216, 223-225
crashes 214-215
Ctrl+Esc 176
current work 137-138
cut 198
    and paste 79

D

Data
    file 39
    files 183
        open 40
    processing 68-69
    Recovery Program 204
date 46, 153
Date & Time 110
Date/Time 50
DDLs 79
default
    screen 205
    setting 97
defaults 189
defragment 86
defragmentizer 207
Delete 25-26, 37, 134
    command 148
Dell 66
Description 20, 36, 39, 131, 134, 193
desktop 29, 35, 98, 111
    clutter 21
    icon 55
    publishing 76
    video 75
Dialog boxes 79
digital 95, 234

speed indicator 86
diminished performance 79
Dingbats 59
disk 72
    access 6
    cache 81
    Checking Software 204
    compression 218-219
    controllers 53
    defragmentation 86, 232
    Defragmentizers 204
    drive 76
        specification 81
diskette formatting 58
document
    embedded 160
    window title bar 102
    windows 98-99
DOS 7, 94, 105-106, 131-133, 139, 161, 173, 184,
    192, 218, 221, 224, 230-232, 237
    application 75
    commands 133
    directory 225
    file name 33, 36
    file path 38
    filename 144
    files 96
    help 79
    name 35, 140
        conventions 140
    path 126, 148
    program 71, 174
        prompt 161
    users 228-229
    wildcards 149
DOS-based 232
dot pitch 84
DoubleSpace 218
download 164
downloading protocols 164
Dr. Watson program 223
drive icon 114
DTP programs 170
DX 77-78
    chip 84
DX2 chip 78
Dynamic Link Libraries 79
Dynamic Link Libraries see also DDL

E

edit 198, 200
EISA 84
    bus motherboards 70
    data bus 77

IDE 80
   machines 88
ellipses (...) 106, 190
embed 199
   icons 157
embedded
   document 160
   object 237
empty group window 21
Enter key 166
error message 221
Everyday 26
   group 54
   window 23-24
executable file 44
Exit 122
   Windows 27, 61, 121, 128
expansion cards 218
extended character 7
extension 44

F

Fast Alt+Tab 112
   Switching 55
file 39
   data 39
   executable 39
   extension 116
   icon 33, 35, 39-40, 140, 148, 152
      create 146, 158
      creating 141-143
      new 38
   opens 37
   organization 138
   server 74, 172
File Manager 22-23, 30, 32, 38, 44, 56-58, 99,
      105, 114, 128, 130, 137, 139-140, 146, 149,
      151, 157-158, 174, 177, 179-180, 185, 188,
      192, 205-206, 211, 219, 222, 224, 232
   close 33
   icon 54
File Menu 19
File Viewer 206
Files 29
   with Extension 44
   group create 34
floats 32
floppy disk 82, 220
   drive 66-67
FontMinder 85
fonts 85, 95, 112, 114, 154, 168, 191
   symbol 168
Free space 67
full-screen 32, 105, 120, 123

Function Keys 192
Functions 194, 197

G

Games group 24
General Protection Failure 214
General Protection Fault 221
General Protection Fault see also GPF
Getting Started 107
GPF 221, 224
Graphic Winmarks test 87
Graphical Users Interface 95
Graphical Users Interface see also GUI
graphics
   applications 84
   commands 71
   format 94
   programs 98
Group
   File box 20
   Icons 120, 122, 124
   window 26, 126, 128
      add 34
      create 34
      rename 34
groups 119
GUI 95-96

H

hard disk 67, 76, 125, 174
   cache 73
   drives 67, 73
hard drive 51, 53, 66, 91, 138
   controller 70
hardware 3, 62, 85, 89, 214
   crash 214
   crashes 219
   upgrades 189
Help 93
   index 192
hidden file 53
high resolution 83
housekeeping 138
HPGL plotter 111

I

IBM 66
icon 30, 36-37, 40, 49, 58, 98, 130, 134
   delete 134
   design 40
   duplicates 38
   highlight 35
   new 42-43
   Write 104

icons 16-19, 21, 24, 26, 33, 42, 118, 129, 204, 239
  copy 54, 128
  create 31
  embed 157
  Installer 129
  leftover 25
  move 54
  Program Manager 139
  ReadMe 22
  set up 137
  Setup 129
IDE
  hard disks 221
  interface 80
image refresh rate 70
import 158
incompatibilities 223
Insert Icon 159
installation program 222
installed 15
Installer 19, 129
Intel 67, 234, 236-237
  chip 67, 230
  upgrade chip 90
Intel-compatible 230
interface 232, 234
  universal 94
intermediate
  application 100
  document 100
  size 99, 121
interrelated pieces 65
ISA machines 88
Item Properties 176

J
jumpers 218

K
key commands 169
keyboard 67
  commands 7, 161, 168
  shortcuts 7, 106, 192
Keyboard and Mouse 192

L
label 158-159
link 44
linked 30, 149
local bus 70, 82
  connects 70
  disk controllers 77
  IDE 80

video 77, 85
  cards 91

M
Mac 240
  operating system 231
machine power 4
macros 161, 194-197
Main 119
  group 24
    window 23, 31, 125
  memory 72
  RAM 79
mainframe 8
mainstream computing 227
Master Pages 194, 196
math co-processor 69
mathematical processing 69
mathematics 68
Maximize 103
  button 14, 31, 100, 102-103, 120
Maximized 99
  application 99-100
  document 100
    windows 99
MCA 228
memory 69, 76
menu bar 49-50, 79
message launch 207
Micro Channel Architecture 228
Micro Channel Architecture see also MCA
minimize 60, 98
Minimize button 14, 49, 100, 103, 120
Minimize on Use 122
MIPS 234
missing files 225
modem 163
Modules 86
monitor 66-67, 77, 84, 216
  non-interlaced 84
  non-flickering 83
MORICONS.DLL 42-43, 133, 149
motherboard 66, 80
  design 70
motherboards 69-70
  EISA bus 70
mouse 67, 94-95, 108-109, 162, 190, 192
  droppings 110
  trails 110
move icons 54
multi-program graphics software bundle 75
multi-threading 230
multimedia extensions 160-161
multiple users 5

245

multitask 51, 105, 173
multitasking 55, 57, 230

N

Nested windows 232
network 74, 172
networking 232
New 19
    program group adding 120
    Size box 53
NeXT company 234
No Title 50
non-local bus cards 91
Norton Desktop 86, 162, 204, 231
    for Windows 203
Norton Tools 232
NOTASSOC.NON 30
Notepad 156, 224
NT applications 233
Num Lock 166
numeric keypad 166

O

Object Packager 157-158, 160, 199
Odds and Ends 24, 26
    group 25
OLE 200
    aware 200
OLE 1.0 237
OLE 2.0 233, 237-238
operating system 89, 228-229, 234
    advanced 230
Optimizer 207
options menu 27, 121
ordinary text 195
outline 197
Outlines 194, 196

P

Paintbrush 60, 103, 162-163
password 206
paste 60, 198
Pastel 108
PATH statement 148
PC configurations 73
PC Tools 86, 162, 203-205, 207, 211, 232
    for Windows 231
    installed 204
Pentium 77, 236
    chip 69, 235
peripherals 70, 216
permanent swap file 180-182
Personal Information managers 185
photo editing programs 162

photomanipulation
    programs 6, 75
    software 74
PIM 185
    icon 187
pixels 162
PLI bus 83
PostScript mode 111
power 74
    supply 217
        fluctuations 215
    surges 215
    users 6, 74
Power PC 235
    chips 235-236
price performance ratio 77
Print File icon 206
printer 110, 216
    driver 85, 110
printing 6
processor 230
    speed 70
PROGMAN.EXE 42-43, 133, 149, 193
Program
    commands 195
    Group 20
        create new 127
    installation routines 222
    Item Properties 36, 38, 41, 43, 131-132,
    134, 152
Program Manager 14, 17, 19, 25-27, 31, 33, 35,
    37, 46, 48, 56, 60-61, 93, 98, 103, 112, 118-
    119, 124-125, 127, 138, 146, 152, 177-178,
    181, 184, 188, 193, 204, 232, 239
    configuration 125
    File menu 35
    group 158
    Help 121
    hide 32
    icons 122, 139
    Main group 55
    Main window 51
    screen 121
    set up 117
    window 120
program swapping 180
PROGRAM.EXE 30
Properties 35, 56, 130, 135, 193
PS/2 computers 228

Q

Quick Launch 206, 208-209, 211
    command 208
    list 209, 211

R

RAM 6, 51, 72-73, 77, 80, 84, 88, 90-91, 94, 105,
172-173, 175, 178-179, 182, 184-185, 214-
215, 228-230
caches 72, 81
memory 67
requirements 75
Read Me 19, 129
files 118, 155
README files 223
rearrange 127
recorder 161-162
Reduced Instruction Set Computing 235
Reduced Instruction Set Computing see also
RISC
refresh rate 84
reinstall 223
renamed file icons 208
Repaginate Now 107
resolution 70
Restore 14, 32-33
button 100, 102-104
RISC 235
chips 236
Run Minimized 56, 133, 175
box 36

S

SafeDelete 206
Save 57, 160, 221
command 106, 219-220
Settings on Exit 27, 121
Save As 57, 103, 191
command 219
Scheduler 207-208
scientific calculator 167
SCRDENGS.DOC 29
screen 13
saver 111
size 117
scripts 194, 196
scroll bar 124
SCSI 80, 84
SCSI-2 80
Search
command 222
for application 126
sectors 221
Select by File Type 115
sensitive material 207
serial port 89
Sets Fonts command 154
Settings 47
menu 50

SetUp 121, 129
Applications 126
SetWindowsSpeed=0.5 97
Shift key 27, 121, 128
Shift-/ 115-116
Shift-Exit Windows 27, 121, 128
Shift-F1 107
Shift-Tab 190
shortcut key combination 133
slash key 166
slider button 109
SmartDrive 85, 215
RAM cache 72
SmartSearch tool 207
software 3, 89
crash 214
crashes 219
errors 214
Sort by Type 115
special
character 59, 168
memory cards 76
speed 67, 74, 91
normal 86
spurious errors 218
Stacker 181, 218
StartUp 46, 54, 119, 153, 185-187, 224
group 24, 47, 54, 152, 184, 186
window 184
storage medium 138
style 194-195
subtopics 197
surge protection 215
suspended animation 105
swap file 52-53, 181-184
permanent 180
SX 78
chip 84
Symbol 59, 168
fonts 167-168
system
clock 154
crash 222
crashes 85
SYSTEM.INI 96

T

Tab 57, 200
Taligent 235
Tape
backup 217
calculator 167
Task List 176
TEMP directory 81-82, 225

temporary files 82
terminals 164, 171
Terminate and Stay Resident 172
Terminate and Stay Resident see also TSR
Test 103
Tile 123
Tiled windows 18
Tiling 17-18, 124-125
time 46, 153
timed backup 219
title bar 102-104, 123
Toolbar 206-207
tools 198
TrueType 86, 112
TSR 172
    program 105
Turbo
    button 86
    switch 87
Tutorial 93, 107

U
Undelete 221
Unformat 221
Uninterruptible Power Supply 216
Uninterruptible Power Supply see also UPS
universal interface 94
UNIX-based software 234
upgrade 76, 90
upgrading 91
UPS 216
    connected tape drive 217
Use 32-Bit Disk Access 53, 184
utilities 232
utility 214
    programs 231

V
ValuePoint series 228
VESA local bus machine 83
VGA screens 162
video
    accelerators 71
    boards 66
    cards 67, 70, 76, 83, 87
    circuitry 70
    circuits 76
    commands 83
    drivers 85
    processing workload 71
view an application 100
virtual memory 51-52, 54, 105, 183-184
    button 52
    creates 94

virtual reality 75
virus 221
    check 207
    scans 220
viruses 220

W
wallpaper 111
whole language 196
WIN 161
WIN.INI file 85, 96
Windows 79
    active 103
    Appearance 159
    application 98, 122, 129
    Clock 46, 154
    Content 158-159
    directory 42, 133
    document 98-99
    empty group 21
    Everyday 23-24
    group 26, 126
    hacker 152
    install 55
    Main 16, 23, 125
    Notepad 152
    NT 173, 229-231, 233-235
        applications 232
    Program Manager 120
    programs 71
    secrets 97
    Setup 125
    StartUp 46
    System directory 223
    Tiled 18
    Work 234
    Write 156
Windows 3.1 231-233
Windows 4.0 231, 233, 237, 239
WINFILE.EXE 140
WingDings 168
WinJet printer card 186
word processor 60, 156
Working Directory 39, 133-134
Wrap Title 112
Write icon 104

Z
Zapf Dingbats 168